Falling:

A Journey of Strength, Survival and Rising

by
L.A. Batista

Copyright © 2025 L.A. Batista All rights reserved.

No part of this publication shall be reproduced, transmitted, or sold in whole or in part in any form without prior written consent of the author, except as provided by the United States of America copyright law. Any unauthorized usage of the text without express written permission of the publisher is a violation of the author's copyright and is illegal and punishable by law. All trademarks and registered trademarks appearing in this guide are the property of their respective owners.

For permission requests, write to the publisher, addressed "Attention: Permissions Coordinator," at the address below.

Publish Your Purpose
141 Weston Street, #155
Hartford, CT, 06141

The opinions expressed by the Author are not necessarily those held by Publish Your Purpose.

Ordering Information: Quantity sales and special discounts are available on quantity purchases by corporations, associations, and others. For details, contact the author at L.A.Batista125@gmail.com

Edited by: Connie Mayse & Anna Heim
Cover design by: Nelly Murariu
Cover Illustration by: Ashley Hernandez
Typeset and E-book design by: Amit Dey

ISBN: 979-8-88797-159-9 (hardcover)
ISBN: 979-8-88797-158-2 (paperback)
ISBN: 979-8-88797-160-5 (ebook)

Library of Congress Control Number: 2024949745

First edition,

The information contained within this book is strictly for informational purposes. The material may include information, products, or services by third parties. As such, the Author and Publisher do not assume responsibility or liability for any third-party material or opinions. The publisher is not responsible for websites (or their content) that are not owned by the publisher. Readers are advised to do their own due diligence when it comes to making decisions.

Publish Your Purpose is a hybrid publisher of non-fiction books. Our mission is to elevate the voices often excluded from traditional publishing. We intentionally seek out authors and storytellers with diverse backgrounds, life experiences, and unique perspectives to publish books that will make an impact in the world. Do you have a book idea you would like us to consider publishing? Please visit PublishYourPurpose. com for more information.

 # Dedication

This book is dedicated to:

My grandmother, whose love and support will be with me always.

My mother, for giving me the gift of faith and teaching me the value of education.

My father, who made my childhood fun, and was always by my side offering support well into my adulthood.

My sons, Christopher and Andrew, my greatest source of pride and my reasons for pushing through feelings of inadequacy. Because of them, I persevered and tried to be the best version of myself.

My husband, Jorge, who I can never thank enough for all he has done and continues to do for me. He has stood beside me through the worst of times. He lifted me up literally and figuratively during my most difficult struggles, allowing me to feel wanted and loved. I'll be forever grateful for his never-ending support during my darkest moments of despair.

To all the friends, coworkers, and strangers who picked me up off the floor, helping me to rise. I will never forget those moments of kindness.

To all the parents who have lost their precious children to SMA.

To all the people and caregivers dealing with the challenges of life with a disability.

Author's Note

Dear reader,

Growing up, I felt like an anomaly because there was no one in my life like me. As I got older, I journaled about my hardships, writing as a way to release my feelings and make sense of what was happening to me. I've tried to be as accurate as possible while writing this memoir. Every story involving others has been verified by someone who was close to me during the time it occurred. I have changed most of the names in this book to provide anonymity to friends and family members.

I wrote this book for those who grew up with a disability, feeling alone in the world; for women in abusive relationships who think they can't make it on their own; for single moms (and dads) struggling to give their children a good life; and for anyone who is struggling with adversity. My hope is that, in reading this book, you will realize that you are not alone in feeling different, misunderstood, or abandoned. Although our struggles may be different, we all yearn to feel accepted and valued. My journey is one of learning to accept who I am and appreciate all I have to give, rather than focusing on what I am unable to do, and to recognize the strength I have, and have always had, despite being physically weak.

We are so much more than our frailties, whether physical, mental, or emotional. As I look back on the turmoil and obstacles that knocked me down, I realize I arose stronger each time. We should not judge ourselves by the moments we fell but by the times we got up, even when it was because someone offered a hand to help us rise. Just remember—you are not alone, and your hardships do not define who you are. You have the ability to rise above whatever life throws your way.

L.A. Batista

Prologue

Falling . . . like the dreams many people have. You are falling off a cliff or rooftop, but just before you hit the ground, you wake up. Your body jerks on the bed as if you have just landed. Your eyes open, then you go back to sleep, comforted by the realization that you were just dreaming. Now, imagine that this is not a dream but a common occurrence.

Envision falling down with no warning. Like a ton of bricks, you slam down so fast, you don't even know it is happening. You rip through your pants and flesh and bruise your knees. You fall while you are walking and talking with your friends or when you are going to place your plate in the sink after eating. Falling because you didn't notice a crack in the sidewalk or a pebble in your path. You fall because someone bumped into you, or someone's bag knocked into you. There are times that you fall for what seems to be no reason at all. You look at the floor for a culprit to blame it on. You require a reason for the occurrence so you can avoid it next time.

Sometimes you know you are too weak to hang on. You push yourself to get through the day, knowing you are on the verge of losing your grip, like a leaf holding on in a windstorm. If you are lucky, you make it through the day unscathed.

Imagine being consumed with thoughts of the earth under you. With every step you take, you think about how to avoid falling, prohibiting you from being able to move about freely. You do everything in your power to prevent it: you wear sensible shoes, scan the ground in front of you, and try to avoid crowds and running children. You get caught off guard when you are living in the moment, forgetting to focus on not falling. You trick yourself into believing that you can control or prevent it, but deep down inside you don't believe this fallacy. You know it will happen again no matter how careful you are.

Sometimes it hurts so badly that you must fight back tears. The worst part is not the physical aspect of falling, but the inability to get up. You are at the mercy of others. The fact that you need someone to actually pick you up is the most humiliating part of it.

There is nowhere to hide, no way out of the helpless situation. You wish that you were invisible, but you are more visible than anyone else around. You are the one who is weak and helpless. You are no longer the independent, strong adult who left the house that morning. It cuts you down and takes away your dignity. You wish you were sleeping safely in bed where you can roll over and tell yourself that it was just that dream again, but you cannot comfort yourself because it isn't a dream. It is a nightmare that doesn't go away and becomes more frequent over time. You are a leaf living in a perpetual season of autumn.

Table of Contents

Author's Note v

Prologue. vii

Chapter 1: Ignorance Is Not Always Bliss 1

Chapter 2: School Days 15

Chapter 3: Diagnosis and Denial 41

Chapter 4: Marriage, Motherhood, and Mayhem. 65

Chapter 5: Moving On 101

Chapter 6: The Road of Single Motherhood 129

Chapter 7: Ceremonies of Passage 149

Chapter 8: Career and Love 155

Chapter 9: Millennial Bride 171

Chapter 10: Working 185

Chapter 11: To do is to be—Socrates To be is to do—Plato. . . 203

Chapter 12: Hope 207

Chapter 13: Rising 215

Acknowledgements 219

About the author 221

Chapter 1

Ignorance Is Not Always Bliss

My parents grew up in Brooklyn in the 1950s. My mother was seventeen when she dropped out of high school in 1960 to marry my father, who was twenty. They rented a two-bedroom railroad apartment in Flatbush, on the second floor, just across the street from our maternal grandmother, Nanny.

My first memory is of the day, a week before my third birthday, when mom brought my sister Megan home from the hospital. Mom walked in carrying Megan, swaddled in a blanket. I stretched my arms up toward her so she could pick me up. Mom looked down at me and walked away, whisking her bundle into her bedroom. I folded my arms and slid down against the wall, crying. Mom felt that, since she had a new baby, it was time for me to stop being carried. But I was different from my sister Mary, who was two years older. I walked slowly and struggled to keep up. I tired easily and fell often. I wanted to be carried when my legs were fatigued. Mom thought that I was lazy and didn't want to spoil me.

As I got older, my symptoms persisted. "What's wrong with her?" The familiar question, whispered by adults or blurted out by children, had gone unanswered by my parents and doctors. At a young age, I noticed that I did things differently. Although I met all my milestones (sitting, standing, and walking) on time, I was unable to physically keep up with my peers. My sisters could walk up the stairs without using the banister to pull themselves up. They could walk much farther and faster than I could without tiring. My hips dropped when I walked. I didn't realize that I walked differently from everyone else until others asked me, "Why do you walk like that?" I needed to rest or hold onto someone to continue walking once I was fatigued. If I didn't rest, my gait turned into a noticeable limp and, eventually, a waddle. When I fell, I had difficulty getting up. I was the different one, the one who had to be waited for; the one who couldn't keep up and who fell frequently. The older I got, the more apparent it became that I wasn't just a clumsy kid. The question that puzzled family, friends, and nosy neighbors began to worry me. As I became aware of my inabilities, I became perplexed and began to ask questions.

When I was about eight years old, I went into Nanny's kitchen. She was scrubbing an article of clothing on an old, rusty washboard in the deep side of her white cast-iron sink. "Nanny, could I have some milk?" I asked. "Of course you can, honey," she replied. She smiled as I drank. It pleased her to see us eat and drink. She often told us stories of the hardships she endured during the Great Depression.

"I was alone with four children and had to wait for checks from your grandfather, who was away at sea. Sometimes the checks were late or didn't come. I didn't always have money for food. When my kids' shoes were worn through, I put cardboard in them to cover the holes because I had no money to buy new ones."

Nanny, an Irish immigrant, worked evenings cleaning office buildings in Manhattan once her children were grown. Grandpa was still in the Navy, but she no longer had to depend on him. She always made sure there was food and fresh milk on hand whenever we visited. Through the way she fussed over us, I got the sense that she wanted to make sure we didn't suffer the way her children had.

After gulping down the cold glass of milk, I handed her the glass and asked, "Nanny, what's wrong with my legs?" My deep brown eyes scanned her pale face as I waited for an answer. As I examined her expression, I watched the smile on her thin lips fade away. Her eyes, the color of the Caribbean Sea, turned into pools of sadness as my words hung in the air like a gloomy cloud that unexpectedly eclipsed the sun. She looked down at me with heartache.

Desperate to mollify me, she explained, "When you were younger, you were sickly and needed to have your tonsils removed. When the doctor was removing them, some poison seeped out, went through your bloodstream, and affected your legs." It doesn't sound like a good explanation, but for a while, it was good to have a reason. I recall telling that story to a few of my classmates when they asked me why I walked the way I did.

Nanny was the one we went to when we wanted to be fussed over. If any of us were sick, she brought us chicken soup, orange juice, cough drops, and other essentials that made us feel special. She always had bandages and ointment for cuts and scrapes. Being a "clumsy" child, I was prone to sprained ankles. Nanny bathed my foot in Epsom salts and then wrapped my ankle in an elastic bandage. She tended to my childhood wounds like a loving nurse, with a sincere look of worry on her face, as if she could feel my pain.

We visited her often and frequently slept over on weekends. We spent most of our time in her dining room. It was adjacent to her kitchen and was the hub of her apartment. A television set sat between two windows at the end of her dining table, on a stand with tall legs. There we did our homework, colored, and played card games like Old Maid when we weren't watching our favorite shows.

On Sunday mornings, she brought us to Mass. I tucked my hand into the fold of her elbow when I needed support while we strolled toward the church. She walked with her head held up and a slight smile of contentment on her mouth. Sometimes I'd hold onto her just because I wanted to feel close to her. When we entered the building, we dipped our fingers into the well of holy water mounted on a wall in the entryway and blessed ourselves. We lit candles at the back of the church and said a prayer for the sick and dearly departed. We then followed her like ducklings down the aisle, genuflecting before filing into the pew after her.

Our neighborhood consisted of apartment buildings and two-family dwellings that were located over small businesses. On our way home, we passed many shops. Nanny often stopped at Michael's Prime Meats on Nostrand Avenue for fresh cold cuts. As we waited for our order, I slid my feet across the floor, making piles of the sawdust that covered it. Next door to Michael's was Jeffery's Bakery. Sometimes we stopped in there for some fresh-baked bread or chocolate eclairs. Even when we didn't stop in the bakery, I loved passing by just to inhale the sweet aroma of the fresh baked goods. It was much more pleasant than the foul smell that emanated from the seafood store that followed. I felt sorry for the fish lying on ice, staring back at me through the store window with their dead eyes and open mouths. It seemed as though they had something to say, but they were silenced as they lay in their frozen beds.

Nanny's apartment was a refuge from some of Mom's rules. We could eat all the junk food we wanted and watch an unlimited amount of television. "Now sit down and watch TV while I make you a nice sandwich," Nanny directed as we entered her dining room. It was a place where we tried to control our bickering. If we forgot, all she had to do was threaten that she wouldn't let us come back and we were on our best behavior.

Mom was always busy. As a housewife, she took pride in making our apartment a home that was always clean and organized. She reupholstered chairs, put up wallpaper, painted, and built bookshelves. She learned to crochet and made afghans, ponchos, scarves, and baby blankets, which she often gave to family and friends as gifts. She talked about how she had taught herself a complicated stitch or how she made an intricate flower that took her days to figure out. Her face beamed with pride as she spoke. I was honored to wear a multicolored poncho to school and bragged to my classmates that she had made it for me. She also enjoyed cooking and often baked bread and pies from scratch. I watched her as she flattened the dough with her rolling pin, adding a bit of flour to keep it from sticking as she created a perfect pie crust.

Mom dabbled in drawing and painting and even taught herself the basics of playing the guitar. If she wasn't cooking or involved in a project, she was reading. When I was about five years old, she went to school in the evenings to learn Spanish. Her thirst for knowledge led her to earn her high school diploma. She eventually continued on to college and then to graduate school. Mom loved learning and was proud of her accomplishments. I often listened to her boast about how she studied all night and got an A on an exam. She talked about solving algebraic equations, memorizing theorems for geometry, and figuring out lengths and angles of triangles in trigonometry. In college, she excitedly discussed things she was learning about in sociology, psychology, and geology, among other subjects. Words like Freudian, socioeconomic, and glacial striations became part of our lexicon as she shared her knowledge at the dinner table. Although she didn't work full-time, she had a couple of part-time jobs over the years. She often used her earnings and her grant money from school to buy new furniture or clothing for us. As an inquisitive child, I followed her around the apartment while she watered her plants, asking her endless questions. I admired her intelligence and wanted to be like her. When I got good grades, she made me feel special by hanging my tests, adorned with golden stars or scripted "Es"—for excellent—on the mantle.

Mom, a devout Catholic, made sure we prayed before meals and before bed. We were taught to say the rosary and make novenas. When we lost an item, we prayed to Saint Anthony, the patron saint of lost things. "Saint Anthony, Saint Anthony, please help me find my keys." If a pet was sick, we prayed to Saint Francis of Assisi. We went to church every Sunday, but I sometimes went with Mom on weeknights while my sisters stayed at home. She would often go to the evening Mass before heading to night school. After Mass, she would walk me halfway home and then rush off to class. We shared a spiritual bond. I felt very close to her during that time.

Mom was the disciplinarian in our family. We had chores to do and rules to follow. We were required to use proper table manners, and as we got older, we were expected to make our beds and take turns washing dishes, setting and clearing the table, and cleaning the bathroom. She was strict about how much television we watched. We were only allowed one hour of television a day, and homework had to be done first. She didn't allow junk food, and we weren't allowed to drink sodas or any sweet drinks. At dinner, we drank milk or tea.

When it came to my "condition," I think Mom thought or hoped that I would outgrow it. At first, she thought I was lazy and just wanted to be carried. "You refused to walk, standing on the sidewalk like a mule. It was difficult to carry you, especially when I was pregnant with your sister." When I got older and asked, "Mommy, why do my legs hurt when I walk, and why is it hard to go up the stairs?" she often answered, "There's nothing wrong with you. You just need to exercise and eat your vegetables." Vitamins and spoonfuls of cod liver oil were other remedies that Mom promoted. Exercise seemed to have the adverse effect. It made me tired and sore. When I was very young, she occasionally rubbed alcohol on my aching legs when I complained of soreness after long walks.

Mom was a great cook but as far as vegetables went, I hated them except for corn and green beans. "If you don't eat your vegetables, you won't get dessert," Mom threatened. Dessert was my favorite part of the meal, so I held my breath and washed the limp broccoli or smelly cabbage down with milk. Other times, I'd make deals with my sisters when Mom walked away. "If you eat my vegetables, I'll give you half of my dessert." If one of them agreed, I quickly slid the unwanted plants onto one of their plates. Having half of the dessert was better than none. I must admit that I reneged a few times, so the wheeling and dealing wasn't an option for long. Many times, I just flat-out refused to eat. It wasn't just the vegetables that I rejected. I hated fish and liver, two other foods that Mom deemed curative.

"If you don't finish your dinner, you will have to stay at this table all night," Mom warned. After the table was cleared, I listened to my sisters playing or laughing and talking in our bedroom while I sat with my head on the table and the plate of cold food next to me. "You are as stubborn as a mule. Go to bed, but you are going to eat it for breakfast," Mom said as she removed the rejected meal. In the morning, I would be relieved to see that there was no sign of her threat being carried out.

Sometimes Dad walked in from work while we were having dinner. As soon as we heard him enter the apartment, we yelled out, "Daddy's home!" We dropped our forks and ran to meet him at the door, greeting him with hugs and sometimes asking him to make a muscle so that we could swing from his arm. After welcoming him home, we sat back at the table to finish our dinner. Dad worked at different companies in the shipping and receiving department. Besides working to support the family, his mission was to make sure we had fun.

On Christmas Eve, my sisters and I lay awake, too excited to sleep. We heard, "Ho, ho, ho, Merry Christmas!" coming from the living room. "Santa is here, Santa is here," we whispered. Then we heard Dad saying, "The girls are asleep, Santa." I shut my eyes tight so that Santa wouldn't think that I was awake and leave coal in my stocking.

"Thank you, Santa, I'll leave these presents under the tree," Dad said. "Merry Christmas, ho, ho, ho," exclaimed Santa. We heard the apartment door open and close as Dad said goodbye to Santa. Megan and I giggled with delight from the bottom bunk that we shared. Mary leaned over from the top bunk and said, "Go to sleep before he comes back and takes the gifts away."

On Christmas mornings, we tore open our gifts, littering the living room floor with mounds of wrapping paper while Christmas carols sung by Johnny Mathis and Nat King Cole played on Dad's record player. We usually got an abundance of presents that included new pajamas, robes, slippers, toys, and board games. Some of my fondest memories are of Dad playing Monopoly and other board games with us on weekends.

The night before Easter Sunday, Dad colored eggs with us then hid them around the apartment for us to find in the morning. We couldn't wait to wear the new dresses, coats, hats, and shoes that Mom picked out for us. We all went to church together dressed in our new clothing. Afterward, our parents would take us to the Brooklyn Botanical Garden. The cherry blossoms were in full bloom, and the greenhouse was full of exotic plants whose names I couldn't pronounce.

To make us feel special on our birthdays, Dad came up with a rule: on our birthdays, we didn't have to do any chores. "Today you are queen for a day. You don't even have to make your bed,." he said.

Mom made all the meals, but Dad sometimes made breakfast on weekends. He cooked grits and eggs or a pot of hot Cream of Wheat cereal on a cold winter's day, but his specialty was pancakes and bacon. The three of us would gather in the small kitchen, handing him ingredients. We watched as he oiled the pan with bacon fat before scooping the batter out with a ladle. We were entertained watching him flip the pancakes up and out of the pan as he laughed and joked.

Dad was an avid music lover. Music always played on the radio. In the evenings, He played records from his vast collection. Sometimes, when company was over on weekends, the music kept us awake. The lyrics from classic doo-wop songs, The Beatles, the Rolling Stones, Nat King Cole, Ella Fitzgerald, Lou Rawls, and many others are embedded in my memory. Dad also listened to classical music, from Beethoven to Mozart. Sometimes he wore headphones and conducted the orchestra with an invisible baton as he pretended to be the maestro.

Growing up in the concrete jungle, the sidewalk was our playground. We played hopscotch and jacks, bounced balls to each other or against buildings, and jumped rope. I could jump a little when jumping solo. We played hand games while singing songs, like "Miss Lucy Had a Baby" and "Miss Mary Mack," in front of our building. If we had a quarter, we walked to the corner store to buy candy, potato chips, or ice cream.

It was a treat to go on family outings. In the summer, we went to Coney Island. As soon as we approached the boardwalk, I could smell the salty air and hear the waves crashing. We played in the sand and collected seashells. Dad asked, "Who wants to get buried?" We'd help him dig the hole, and one of us would get in with only our heads exposed. The cool, damp sand that covered us in our shallow graves provided a break from the hot sun. When we were ready to get out, we broke free and ran into the water to wash the sand off.

When Dad was ready to go for a swim, he got up and sprinted toward the cold ocean water, then dove into the waves. Dad was a good swimmer. I remember asking, "Daddy, can you take me out over my head?" I wrapped my arms around his neck while he towed me out into the deep water. I loved the feeling of weightlessness in the water. Mom didn't swim, but I have memories of us floating in the shallow water together, with sun-kissed faces as we held hands while the waves gently rocked us. We often stayed at the beach until dusk. As evening approached, the squawks of seagulls could be heard as they descended on the beach to scavenge for leftover morsels. Walking in the sand at the end of the day was a bit difficult, but holding onto Dad's arm helped me trudge on.

Sometimes Dad took us out to give Mom a break so she could study in peace. Occasionally, we would head to Coney Island just for the amusement park. We rode on the Wonder Wheel, the bumper cars, and my favorite, the Himalaya, which went around a track so quickly while playing loud music. After slowing down, it started up again going backwards. People gathered around the ride to watch and listen to the loud music and blaring sirens. Once, the song "Love Rollercoaster" by the Ohio Players was blaring from the speakers and we begged him to let us ride it. He took us on the Cyclone. I thought I was going to fall out of the seat and crash to my death. I never rode it again, but I had bragging rights that I had ridden one of the oldest, scariest rollercoasters of that time.

Mary loved going into Spook-A-Rama, the haunted house ride. I buried my face in Dad's chest during the entire ride, peeking out between my fingers at witches, skeletons, and mummies, all the while hearing him laugh at what I thought were the most frightful things on earth. Dad always tried his hand at winning a prize. Sometimes he attempted to be the first to pop a balloon that protruded from a clown's mouth by filling it with a water gun, or he'd throw rings at bottles placed closely together, hoping one would land around the neck. We stood near him watching and cheering for him. Occasionally he would win, and it was up to us to remember whose turn it was to get the prize.

We went to Nathan's for their world-famous hot dogs and thick, soft fries smothered with cheese. Dad always ordered a half dozen clams and squirted lemon juice and hot sauce on them. I watched him scrape them out of their shells with his teeth. I tried one once, but it slipped from side to side in my mouth when I tried to chew it, so I swallowed it whole. Before going home, we'd get some cotton candy. I enjoyed watching it grow on the stick as the vendor turned it around the cylinder. I loved how a large fluffy piece would be reduced to a small bit of hard sugar in my mouth.

Another favorite place we frequented was Prospect Park. It was a treat to have the opportunity to be near nature. Our usual landscape of brick buildings was replaced by towering trees with leaves cascaded in different hues of green. The gray concrete floor we were accustomed to became a plush green carpet.

In the spring, we visited the zoo. We fed peanuts to the elephants through the thick bars that separated us. We watched the lions and tigers pace back and forth in their cages and viewed the bears in their enclosure from above. The monkey house was filled with loud screeches and smelled so bad that I tried to hold my breath until we passed through it. We observed the seals swimming happily and sunbathing on the rocks. After making our rounds of all the sections, we stopped at the zoo restaurant for lunch.

There was a sign at the entrance that read, "Animals, Please Don't Feed the People." When the weather was warm, we sat at tables outside the restaurant. Bees gathered around us following the sweet smell emanating from our sodas. Mary often tried to pet the bees that perched on her straw or landed on the table. Dad smiled and warned, "*Be* careful, that *bee* might sting you," then laughed at his use of the homonyms.

After lunch, Dad put us on the carousel and bought us boxes of Cracker Jacks. My sisters and I couldn't wait to rip open our boxes and search for the mysterious prize buried beneath the peanuts and caramel-covered popcorn. During the summer, he took us to the lake to feed the ducks and ride paddleboats. We rolled down grassy knolls until we got dizzy and rested in fields of clovers. "Who can find a four-leaf clover?" Dad asked. It was a difficult task, but we enjoyed the challenge. We searched for what felt like hours. Occasionally, one of us would find one. "It will bring us luck," he said before putting it in his wallet, tucked between the plastic that held photos. It stayed in his wallet until the next time one of us found one. I watched as he removed the dry, faded one and replaced it with a fresh, vibrant one.

In the fall, we stomped on crisp leaves, enjoying the crunching sound they made under our feet. Mary took delight in knocking us down onto piles of dry leaves. One year, we got roller skates for Christmas. They were the ones that you wore over your shoes and used a key to tighten. My sisters were able to skate the way Dad showed them, sliding one foot in front of the other. It was difficult for me to keep my balance, but I was able to skate a little if I held onto his arm.

As we strolled through the park, my legs grew tired and sore, so we rested on benches along the path. We invented a game called "Mind

My Seat." Once Dad made his way toward the bench, we would rush to his side to get a seat next to him. The two of us who got a seat next to him were the lucky ones. The one left out would try to lure one of the lucky two away from the bench and attempt to rush back to the seat of status. Some lures we used included, "Come here, I see a squirrel," or "Can you come with me to the water fountain?" Dad laughed as we tricked and connived to get someone off the bench. "Move your feet, lose your seat," we squealed. Dad came up with a rule: If we said, "Mind my seat," we could walk away from the bench, free to wander about until we wanted to sit again.

If I got tired and there weren't any benches around to rest on, Dad would give me a piggyback ride for a few minutes. Sometimes my sisters insisted, "I want a piggyback ride, too, Daddy!" He gave them short piggyback rides from one lamppost to the next. After a long day at the park, it was nice to rest my legs in the car on the way home.

One autumn day, we were at the park with Mom and Dad. We came upon craggy hills that we called mountains. The foliage was transforming from green to bright yellow, mocha, orange, and crimson. "Let's climb the mountain," Mary yelled. I was weary from walking through the park. As I toiled toward it, I clutched Dad's arm. I was not looking forward to climbing. I wanted to say, "I don't want to climb the mountain," but they were already running toward it in anticipation of conquering it. The rocks and tree roots protruding from the ground created a hazard. I grabbed onto Dad's arm tighter and pulled on it as I tried to climb. I tugged on him more and more as we ascended. I watched as the wind sent the weak, frail leaves that could no longer sustain their grip spiraling to the ground. I was afraid that I would lose my grip and go tumbling down the hill along with them. My sisters were already near the top. We were halfway up when I needed to stop and rest. Dad bent down and offered me a piggyback ride. I looked up to see Mom looking down at us, saying, "Don't carry her; she can do it. If Megan can do it, so can she." Although Megan was younger, she was much stronger than me. I felt bad that Mom didn't approve of Dad carrying me, but getting relief was more vital. I began to sense that Mom and I had become adversaries when it came to my condition, while Dad remained an ally. As I got older, Dad didn't carry me anymore, but he always walked slowly with me and let me hold his arm. When I became weary, he stopped to rest with me. Most times just standing still for a minute or so was enough of a rest to revive my muscles.

Mom didn't drive, so if we went on outings to Prospect Park with her, we walked. It was a little under a mile away just to get to the entrance. Mom didn't slow down her pace. I felt she disapproved of me walking slowly. As usual, I'd end up lagging behind. My sisters were able to keep up, so they would all be ahead of me. Mom waited at the end of each block until I caught up. When we walked down long avenues, the distance between us grew so great that I'd lose sight of them. When I got tired, I leaned against a fence, a lamppost, or a parked car for a rest. I felt lonely and left out as I trekked on unaccompanied. I wondered what they were talking or laughing about. "Will you walk slowly with me?" I sometimes asked one of my sisters. Sometimes one of them would walk with me, but most times, I lagged behind alone. When I did catch up to them, I hoped that the traffic light would be red so I could rest a little before continuing to walk. When they reached our block, they no longer waited for me. They went inside the building as I trailed behind. By the time I got home, I had walked over two miles. The stairs leading to our apartment were yet another hurdle for me to conquer. I held onto the banister and pulled myself up one step at a time. I was happy to be home where I could rest my achy muscles.

As the years rolled on, it became obvious that good wishes, vegetables, and exercise weren't helping. I wasn't going to outgrow whatever was causing my muscle weakness. The older I got, the more I complained and pushed for answers. Mom continued insisting that there was nothing wrong. Eventually, she began saying that I was making it all up because I just wanted attention. No one was willing to go against Mom and her theory—not verbally, at least. Dad and Nanny let me know they believed me whenever they walked slowly or offered their arm for me to hold onto.

I knew that something *was* wrong with me, and I wasn't a liar. I felt alone dealing with this. There was no one like me. No one really understood what it was like to struggle to do ordinary things. I didn't understand what was happening to me. *Why me? Why only me?* I wondered. I tried to do what Mom did and ignore it, but every time I fell and couldn't get up or whenever I faced a flight of stairs, I was reminded that I wasn't like everyone else. I was a child with no power. I was silenced, like the fish that lay in the seafood store with their mouths open, without voices.

Chapter 2

 ## School Days

"Tick, tock, it's seven o'clock, soon school bells will be ringing," Dad sang before heading out to work. We slowly emerged from our slumber and got dressed for school. Mom was always home when we returned. Once we were settled in and started our homework, she began to prepare dinner.

"Hey, I got a riddle for you. Who's buried in Grant's tomb?" Dad asked at the dinner table. *Is this a trick question? Maybe it's Grant's wife. Who else would be buried in his tomb*, I wondered. "You give up? It's Grant! Grant is buried in Grant's tomb," he informed us while laughing. "Oh, daddy, that's so corny," Mary and I said in unison.

"One of my professors gave me a B on my paper. I argued and showed him where I got my information from. The points that I made in my paper were backed up by the reading assignments. After going back and forth, he finally changed my grade to an A-," Mom shared.

"How was your day?" The question was directed at us children in general. "Megan got in trouble for not bringing in her homework and Mary got a 70 on her math test," I blurted out. "Oh boy, you could be a newscaster or a sports announcer like Howard Cosell," exclaimed Dad. "Or you could be a lawyer. The defendant will confess just to get you to stop talking," Mom added.

Everyone at the table laughed. I lowered my head in embarrassment thinking, *I'll show them. I'll stop talking. I'll never talk again, and they will beg me to talk.* But five minutes later I was chatting up a storm.

Besides being loquacious, I was always a fast learner and a good student. I reveled in the knowledge that good grades pleased Mom. One year, Dad said, "Whoever gets the best report card can get anything they want." At the end of that year, he took me to a jewelry shop where I picked out a fourteen-karat gold ring with a blue-green heart-shaped birthstone in the center. The ring and my gold cross, given to me by Nanny on my first Holy Communion Day, were my most prized possessions.

We attended Holy Cross Catholic School. The walk to school consisted of going down a long avenue and across three blocks. The trip doesn't seem too long, but it was a wearisome journey for me, especially during the winter months. One snowy day on our way to school, Mary suggested that we stop in the church on our way to school. She wanted to take her galoshes off before we entered the school building. She was worried about being seen by her peers wearing the ugly rubber coverings. While we were there, we lit a candle and said a prayer, then went to class via a side entrance at the front of the church that led to the schoolyard. From that day on, it became a shortcut for me that provided a place to warm up and rest for a minute or so before going to class.

On a blustery winter day, I was walking to school alone. The wind was fierce and frigid. It pushed me from behind, causing me to walk a little faster. I leaned my back against it to prevent it from throwing me forward. When I turned the corner, the wind was in front of me. I pressed against it with all my might to prevent the gusts from knocking me down. I felt as naked as a bare winter tree as it whipped up under my coat and uniform, encircling my thin, frail legs. I prayed on my way to the church, *Please God, help me make it to your house. My legs are so tired, and I need to sit and rest. I'll offer up my suffering for someone who is sick.* My head was lowered to shield my face from the cruel blast of the icy wind.

Just before reaching my place of refuge, I heard a voice yelling. "Every day you come through here after I mop the floors and dirty them again. I don't want you walking through the church anymore. Walk through the street to get to school like everyone else."

It was the church janitor. He was a tall lanky man with salt-and-pepper hair. There were dark voids in his mouth where teeth once resided. His zygomatic bones protruded like sharp mountaintops, creating deep valleys where cheeks belonged. He stood in front of the church doors, prohibiting entry. His words were harsh and demanding. I stood there powerless as he chastised me. I wanted to say, *you can't tell me not to enter God's house*. After all, the church was open. I wanted to explain, *my time here is for me to talk to God and to rest my legs that are frozen and weary from the harsh cold*. I wanted him to know that I was fighting the wind and could be knocked down by its cruelty at any moment. I wanted him to understand that I wasn't like everyone else who didn't need to rest, but I was silenced by his authority. I wished that I could defy him by walking past him and entering the Lord's house. My eyes welled up as he stood guard, protecting his spotless floors. After his sermon was over, I retreated. As I turned away and walked toward the school, warm, salty streams gushed down my frosty cheeks, pooling in the corners of my lips. Once again, I was silenced by the authority of adults.

Mom didn't want us sitting around idle during the summers, so she enrolled us in the Police Athletic League (PAL). We attended from 1971-73, the years I was between eight and ten years old. We went on trips to beaches, pools, and parks. Once we went to Liberty Island to see the Statue of Liberty. When we arrived, a counselor brought me to an elevator. I was disappointed when I realized that the elevator only brought us up to the top of the pedestal. "We are only at her feet?" I asked. The counselor laughed and said, "We will have to climb to the top of her crown." There were 354 steps, the equivalent of twenty stories to climb. Taking the elevator saved me about 100 steps. The steps were narrow and winding. There were small, built-in ledges that served as seats for those who needed to rest. I sat a few times on my way up. When I finally got to the top, I got to peer through the openings of her crown and enjoy the well-deserved prize of views of Manhattan Island and New York Harbor.

I thought about the story Nanny told me. "When I was seventeen, I left Ireland. I took a ship to America and landed at Ellis Island." I tried to imagine her as a young teenager being greeted by Lady Liberty on her way to Ellis Island with her valise in hand and dreams of a better life. Gravity made the descent from Lady Liberty's crown easier. My legs were very sore for a couple of days afterward, but it was an experience I was glad to have had.

When we went on outings, I didn't look forward to them as the other kids did. Before each trip, anxiety set in. I was already fatigued from the walk to the center. I knew what was coming—the lengthy walks down several avenues to the train and the dreaded climb up the subway stairs on the way back to the center. It was a combination of anticipating the soreness and fatigue I would feel physically and knowing that I wouldn't be able to keep up with the group. It also meant bringing attention to my lagging. The attention brought on questions like, "What's wrong with her?" or "Why does she walk like that?"

One day, we were going on a trip to Manhattan Beach. We stood in front of the center, waiting for the counselors to collect our permission slips. I felt the hot sun on my face and the soft, warm breeze in my hair. I held a brown paper bag that contained a peanut butter and jelly sandwich and a peach. I wore a bright yellow dress trimmed with embroidered white daisies and matching shorts underneath. I felt pretty in my outfit, but despite my sunny attire, there was a dark cloud of worry hovering over me. I always loved going to the beach, but when I went with my family, Dad drove us there.

This arduous trip was taking the fun out of it. I looked around at the other girls and envied their carefree attitudes. They were smiling, talking, and getting excited to leave, while my thoughts were filled with dread. As we left the center, one of the counselors positioned themselves in the front of the line, leading the way, one was in the middle, and another was at the end to make sure no one got lost or left behind. They lined us up in size order, which put me toward the front of the line. We began walking, and one by one, the kids behind me started to pass me. I slowly found myself at the end of the line. The counselor who was at the end had the responsibility of walking with me and trying to get me to catch up to everyone else, but the longer I walked, the more exhausted I became, making it an unrealistic goal. As I lumbered on, the risk for falling increased with every step. The gap between us and the group would become wider and wider. They waited for us to catch up. When I caught up to them, they'd start walking again. I thought it was unfair that they got to rest. I was so exhausted. I felt bad that I was holding everyone up and wished I were home and didn't have to go on the trip. When we finally arrived at the beach, we laid our towels, sheets, or blankets on the sand, creating a patch quilt of different colors and shapes. I was happy to sit down and rest.

The sun scorched the sand, sending girls running straight into the ocean or hopping from one piece of fabric to another until they reached refuge on the cool, wet sand near the shore. Getting into the water was the best part for me. It was a place where gravity didn't threaten me. I could float, jump, and walk without worry. *Maybe I was meant to be a mermaid,* I thought.

When exiting the water, I watched the waves crashing and foaming. I had to be careful, because they had the power to buckle my knees as they pushed against the back of my legs. If they succeeded, I'd tumble around at the shoreline, unable to get up—especially if more waves attacked me while I was down. I'd make my way to deeper water (waist-high), stand up, and try again. I had to time it just right so that the waves crashed at my waist or at my ankles. Once I made it to the shoreline, my toes grasped for solid ground as the retreating water stole the sand from under my feet. By this time, I was safe from the wrath of the waves. With my feet wearing shoes of wet sand, they were protected from the burning ground as I made my way back to the sheet that I shared with my sisters.

After a couple of hours at the beach, the counselors began making announcements. "Okay, girls, no more going in the water. Time to dry off; we are going to leave soon." The worry started to build as I thought about the long, tiresome trip back to the center. My legs were fatigued from walking on sand and fighting the pull of the tide. On our way back, my legs gave out. No longer surrounded by the buoyancy of the sea, I sank to the ground like the shells that blanketed the ocean floor. Linda, the counselor who was with me, helped me up, then called Speedy over. Speedy was a tall, thin Puerto Rican with a mop of dark, curly hair on his head. He got his nickname because of the quickness of his long legs.

"Speedy, she fell, and she's having a hard time keeping up." Speedy bent down and said, "Climb on top of my shoulders." Once I was on his shoulders, I cupped my hands under his chin. He held onto my knees as my legs dangled in front of his chest. Speedy carried me all the way to our destination. I remember how wonderful it felt to rest my aching muscles. After that first time, he carried me on every trip. He looked for me before we began our excursions. Sometimes I would hear comments from the other girls. "Hey Speedy, I'm tired. Can you carry me? or "What's wrong with her? Why do you always carry her? Why can't she walk?"

Speedy never answered them, and the comments didn't bother me at all. I felt relieved to not have to walk. I felt special sitting on top of his shoulders. Instead of being the one lagging behind, I was the one in the front of the line, way up high with the best views. I pretended that I was important, like the queen of Egypt being carried on a litter, like in *The Ten Commandments* movie. I never asked him to carry me. I wouldn't dare. If Speedy was busy counting heads or organizing the groups and forgot about me, I walked until he noticed, or someone reminded him that I was lagging behind.

Eventually he called my mother to share his concerns. I'm sure a question arose along the lines of, "What is wrong with your daughter?" Speedy told me that Mom said there was nothing wrong with me. I put my head down without words to defend myself. I never took it for granted that Speedy would carry me, but he always did. He made camp bearable, and because of that, I grew very fond of him.

Around that time, I had a recurring nightmare that a monster was chasing me. I tried to scream so that my dream would end more quickly, but I was never able to because my mouth always felt glued shut. I wished that I could scream like the women in the horror movies when Frankenstein or the werewolf came upon them. I woke up telling myself that the next time I had a bad dream, I should try to scream, and the scream would end the nightmare and send Dad rushing into my room to comfort me by giving me a St. Joseph aspirin and telling me that everything was okay, like he did when I occasionally fell out of bed. The next time that I had the nightmare, I reminded myself that it was only a dream and that if I screamed, I would wake up. I stopped running and turned toward the monster. I tried to scream but my lips were cemented shut. *Just open your mouth*, I told myself. In the dream I saw myself turn and open my mouth, but no sound was able to escape because inside my mouth was a brick wall.

I stopped trying to scream my way out of bad dreams. Instead, I told myself, *it's only a dream and you can change it*. When I fell in a dream, I told myself, *you can get up and run*. Sometimes, I'd dream that I could fly. I started to manipulate my dreams. I dreamed that I had snowy, white angelic wings that would protrude from my shoulders upon command, allowing me to fly away while spectators below admired me as I soared above them.

One of the shows that I loved watching at Nanny's apartment was *I Dream of Jeannie*. I often fantasized that I could find a genie bottle on the beach or that I had the magical powers of a genie. Sometimes I wished that I could blink my eyes and make myself appear at the top of the staircase or when I was walking slowly behind everyone, I could blink myself in front of them. I daydreamed about different things that would make my life easier, like having a flying carpet for when I was tired of walking. I even wished that I could make my mother have my condition just for one day. I didn't want her to have it to punish her. I wanted her to know how it felt so she would understand what I was going through and believe me.

As I got older, I outgrew daydreams and fantasies. I had to find another way to cope with my feelings of inadequacy. One Good Friday at church, as the priest was performing the Stations of the Cross, I concluded that God must have given me this thing as my cross to bear. If Jesus could endure such suffering, I could deal with mine, which was minute in comparison. I began to rely more on prayer to help me deal with my affliction. When I felt fatigued from walking, I'd pray, *Jesus, please help me make it without falling. Help me to make it to the next corner. I'll rest at the stop sign.* On windy days I'd pray, *help me make it to the lamppost or to the next tree.* I'd hold on until the strong gust passed. Most of the time I'd make it, so I believed that God was helping me. If I fell, I thought maybe I wasn't concentrating when I prayed. I'll pray harder next time, I told myself.

With warm weather and the promise that Mother Nature would be less pugnacious, we were allowed to go into the school yard for recess. The knowledge that spelling tests and math quizzes would soon be a distant memory was accompanied by an unspoken excitement. Girls were jumping rope, singing, "All in together, girls. How do you like the weather, girls? January, February, March, April . . ." while boys bounced handballs against the wall.

I avoided my classmates who chose to play tag or run relay races. I politely said, "No, thank you," when asked to play jump rope. I knew that I would probably fall if I tried. One day, I wandered around the school yard until I found Megan, who was in first grade. I saw her with her friend, snuck up behind them, and tickled them. As I walked back to my side of the yard, I heard my sister's classmate say, "I like your sister." It was easy to get little kids to like you. The older ones expected more from you. As I made my way back, a couple of girls rushed over to me with desperate looks on their faces.

"Will you play jump rope with us, please? We need one more person to turn the rope."

"Okay," I agreed.

I took delight in watching them jump over the rope as I whipped it around them. I watched their legs and marveled at the way they jumped effortlessly. I wondered what it must be like to jump and run without worrying about falling or getting too tired to finish.

"Okay, it's your turn," one of the girls said as she approached me to take the end of the rope. "No, thanks; I don't feel like jumping today," I answered. "Are you sure?" they asked in unison. I smiled and nodded. "I have a stomachache," I lied. "Oh great, she can be a steady ender."

The "steady ender" was a safe role to play. I continued to turn for them as more girls joined in. I watched their legs (chubby legs, skinny legs, short legs, tall legs, pale legs, ashy legs, brown legs, and tan legs), all jumping as if gravity did not exist for them. "Strawberry shortcake, cream on top, tell me the name of your sweetheart. Does it begin with A, B, C, D . . ." I felt like I was part of the fun as I sang along with them.

Avoiding jumping rope was one way to dodge falling, but I couldn't escape it altogether. I was walking across the classroom when I was in the sixth grade. I might have been coming back from sharpening my pencil or throwing something in the trash when suddenly, without any warning, I heard my bones crashing down against the wood floor. It was so loud that it caught the attention of the entire class. The rustling of papers, the tapping of pencils, and the quiet murmur of my classmates' voices came to a halt. The silence that followed was horrifying. There I was lying on the floor, and everyone was looking and waiting for me to get up, but I just stayed there immobilized because I wasn't near anything to hold on to. My head lay on one arm and the other covered my face. My eyes were closed. I dared not open them. I kept thinking that I wished this was one of my bad dreams that I could change or wake up from. Tears seeped out of my eyes creating tiny pools under me. I could smell the dust on the hardwood floor beneath me. I couldn't bear to face the others. I didn't want them to view me as helpless. I thought that maybe if I stayed there long enough, they would think that I fainted. If I fainted, they would understand why I fell. But if I got up and crawled over to a desk and used it to pull myself up, they would think there is something wrong with me. They would ask questions I didn't have answers to. I must have been there for about thirty seconds, but time slowed down to a halt, stretching into what felt like an eternity. I had stayed there too long to get up now.

My teacher came over and lifted me off the floor, my face still sheltered by my arm. Realizing that I was just embarrassed, she took me outside of the classroom and told me to sit on a chair that was against the wall. "Do you want Blanca to come out and sit with you for a while?" she asked. "Okay." I answered as I rubbed my tears away with the sleeve of my shirt. Blanca was one of my close friends. After talking to her for a minute or so, we walked back into the class together. The other kids acted like nothing happened and I did the same.

In the seventh grade, we had a choice between participating in gym and tutoring first graders. I, of course, chose tutoring, especially since I dreamed of becoming a teacher one day. When I was younger, I played teacher with Megan. We lined up our dolls and stuffed animals in rows in front of her blackboard. We handed out papers and pencils and sent the naughty student (usually the monkey) to the principal's office (Mary's room). Now I was able to play teacher with real kids and loved doing it.

I was twelve, going on thirteen, when I started the eighth grade. It was my last year at Holy Cross. The thought of high school scared me. Everything was changing. I had gotten my period a month before school started. I wasn't a little kid anymore. I was becoming a woman—or at least my body was. Mom told her best friend, Joan, that I got my period. When she came over to visit, she said,

"Welcome to the club." I wasn't sure I wanted to belong to that club. I wasn't ready to stop being a kid. Megan and I shared a bedroom, and Mary had a small room at the end of the apartment for herself. Once I "developed," as Mom called it, Megan was put in the smaller room by herself, and Mary was moved into the bigger room with me. I felt ashamed and uncomfortable in my skin. Taking Megan away felt like a punishment. We got along well and loved playing with each other. Mary was a moody teenager and wasn't much fun at the time. Why did I have to change? It was another thing my body did without my permission.

That year we moved across the street into the apartment above Nanny. The two apartments were located over a laundromat. It was great sharing the two-family dwelling with her. We had the building to ourselves and were able to stop in at Nanny's whenever we wanted. However, this meant that I had to climb two flights of stairs to get to our third-floor apartment. When I got home from school, I looked at the long, steep flight of stairs with dread, knowing that there was yet another flight beyond that was waiting for me to conquer. My heavy, textbook-filled bag made climbing the stairs extremely difficult, but I could take my time and go up slowly, resting when needed. If my sisters were around, I'd ask them to carry my books up for me. If I was very tired and no one was around to carry it, I'd leave it in the vestibule and ask one of my sisters to get it for me later.

The same problem persisted at school. Once we entered the building, we were corralled into the stairwell. I stood to the side and watched my classmates run like a herd of caribou being chased by a lion. The sound of their feet pounding against the steps boomed like thunder. I thought that if we were a herd of caribou, I would be the slow and weak prey that was caught while the rest got away safely, like the ones we watched on nature shows. After they were up the stairs and out of sight, I could struggle in privacy. I threw my book bag up a step or two in front of me, then I used the banister to pull myself up to it. Once I reached it, I continued throwing it up until I got to the top.

One day my teacher, Mrs. McGrath, noticed that my seat was empty. She stepped out into the hall to see where I was. She watched as I lumbered up the staircase. Embarrassed when she saw me, I smiled and tried to hurry up.

The next day I was summoned to the principal's office. Sister Mathew Mary was a stern principal who didn't smile much. I nervously walked into her office, wondering what I had done wrong. When I entered, she was sitting behind a large wooden desk. There was a framed photo of a pope on the wall and a small statue of the Blessed Mother on a table in the corner. Sister was wearing a black habit; her veil was trimmed in white, and she wore a chain with a large cross around her neck. She asked me to have a seat.

"Your teacher is concerned about you. She said she saw you throwing your book bag up the stairs. Can you tell me why you were doing this?"

"It's hard for me to walk up the stairs. My book bag is heavy, so I can't carry it and go up at the same time," I explained.

The next day I was called to her office again.

"I called your mother and asked her why you are having trouble climbing the stairs. She said that you are doing it for attention."

"I'm not trying to get attention. I do it at home too. Sometimes, I ask one of my sisters to carry it for me," I informed her.

"I'm going to give you another set of textbooks. This way you can leave one set in school and the other at home, so you will only have to carry your binder back and forth."

I realized that behind the stern look and forced smile, Sister was genuinely kind. I also knew that her helping me meant she believed me. Walking to and from school and up the stairs was so much easier without the heavy textbooks weighing me down.

Getting good grades had always been a way to offset my physical shortcomings. It gave Mom something to be proud of and gave me a self-esteem boost. As I got older, good grades weren't enough to mask my deficiencies. I was always well behaved, but that year my grades slipped, and I went through a period of acting out in class.

I answered my teacher flippantly once and got a laugh from my classmates. I liked the reaction. Mrs. McGrath called me "bold and brazen." Once she stepped out of the room for a minute and told us not to talk while she was gone. I wrote on a piece of paper, crumbled it up, and yelled, "Airmail!" before throwing it across the room to my friend Brenda, eliciting laughter from my peers. I felt like a rebel and enjoyed it. I taught Brenda how to sign the alphabet so that we could communicate without talking. We would sign to each other behind the teacher's back. On another occasion, I let a girl named Denise put some blue eyeshadow on me in the cafeteria. While Mrs. McGrath checked my work, I made sure to blink enough for her to notice the eye makeup, which was not part of the school attire. I was sent home with a note because of that. On another occasion, I was wearing a gold metal choker around my neck and decided it would be fun to connect it to my earring. When the teacher asked me to come up to the blackboard, I flipped the huge hoop back and forth when I turned my head, causing the class to laugh. Mrs. McGrath asked me why I was acting out. I didn't know why, or maybe I just couldn't articulate it. I think I was trying to be seen as the clown, not the girl who walked differently or struggled up the stairs.

"Until you can act like part of the class by following the rules, you will be separated from your classmates." Mrs. McGrath moved my seat up at the front of the room near her desk. I continued to be the class clown for a couple of months but eventually got tired of being a rebel. After a couple of weeks of good behavior, Mrs. McGrath asked, "Are you ready to join the class?" I promised to behave and was allowed to move my seat back into one of the rows with the rest of the class. In June, I graduated from Holy Cross as part of the bicentennial class of 1976.

I started high school at Erasmus Hall the following September. Mom walked me to school on my first day and left me at the gates on Bedford Avenue. I found my way around by asking for directions. The large high school was so different from the small private school I was used to. Most of my friends from Holy Cross went on to Catholic high schools or specialized public high schools. My best friend from eighth grade, Gladys, was the only person I knew from Holy Cross. We weren't in any classes together but sometimes we met at lunch. Whenever we had a spare dollar; we'd rush to the record shop to buy one of the top 40 hits after school.

I was happy to see the school had an elevator. I got in once and smiled at the operator, but he told me to get out. I didn't even think of asking if I could get permission to use it. Despite the challenge of going up the stairs, I adjusted well. I met new friends and earned good grades.

We moved out of Flatbush to a neighborhood called Kensington in April 1977. Our new residence was in a large forty-eight-unit building with an *elevator*. Our apartment was 1,000 square feet, with five rooms and one and a half baths. There were windows in every room—thirteen in total. All the rooms were spacious, with hardwood floors. The living and dining rooms had archways and stucco walls, giving the apartment a Spanish feel. For the first time, I had windows in my bedroom, and more importantly, I didn't have to walk up the stairs. My sisters and I were excited to explore the neighborhood and make friends.

On Easter Sunday, just a few days after we moved, Mom's father died. Mom didn't want Nanny to be alone, so she convinced her to move into our building when an apartment became available. Within a year, she was living two floors above us. It was great having her close to us again. She met a woman named Nelly, who lived on the fifth floor, above Nanny. The two Irish widows became best friends.

That first summer, there was a massive heatwave that caused a huge power outage (the blackout of '77) that crippled New York City for a couple of days. We were hanging out in front of the building, hoping to catch a cool evening breeze as a relief from the sweltering heat. I noticed a girl about my age going into the building. After seeing each other a few times, we became friends. Tina lived on the sixth floor. We quickly realized that we both came from Flatbush, had attended

Erasmus Hall, and were starting school at Franklin Delano Roosevelt High School in September. We instantly became best friends. We wore the same size clothing and shoes and enjoyed borrowing from each other. We talked about boys, listened to records, and watched Spanish novellas together. I also got close to her sister Lydia. Lydia and I were fourteen and Tina was fifteen. When I told them about my "condition," they were sympathetic. Tina suffered from asthma and understood what it was like having physical limitations. Lydia was protective of me. If anyone laughed at me when I fell, she would tell them not to laugh or she would kick their asses.

Tina's mom, Angela, was born in Puerto Rico and didn't speak much English, but all her children were bilingual including her sons, Hector and Luis. I loved listening to them speak Spanish and envied them. Although Dad was half Puerto Rican, he was raised by his African American mom and never acquired the language. Since I looked Spanish, Puerto Ricans and other Hispanics often approached me speaking in Spanish. When I told them that I didn't speak Spanish, they looked bewildered. I felt bad disappointing them.

I listened to the salsa music they played during the holidays and family celebrations. I learned about the special dishes they cooked for the holidays, like *pernil* (roasted pork shoulder) served with *arroz amarillo con gandules* (yellow rice with green pigeon peas). I watched Angela make *pasteles* (pork encased in a green plantain masa wrapped in banana leaves) for Christmas. The smell of *sofrito* (sauteed blend of onions, peppers, and garlic) made my mouth water when I entered their apartment. I was attracted to the rich culture and wanted to be part of it. I took Spanish in school and learned a little just by hanging around them.

Tina and I went to school together when our schedules permitted. We tried to go in early so that I had time to walk slowly to the bus stop. The bus stop was only one avenue away, but when the weather was cold, windy, or icy, I needed extra time. Getting on the public buses was not easy for me. If the bus got very close to the curb, I could step up on the first step, which was lower than the others. Once

I was on the first step, I used the handles to pull myself up onto the higher steps. Since the bus stop was in front of the bank, customers sometimes blocked the bus stop with their cars. When this happened, the bus driver would stop out in the middle of the street, making the bottom step too high for me to climb. I had to stand there and let the bus go by and wait for the next one. The kneeling buses were new back then. Not all of them had the kneeling feature. If I got a kneeling bus, I'd ask the driver to lower the step for me if it wasn't near the curb.

One time I tried to climb up the step on the new kneeling bus, but it was too high because he had stopped in the middle of the street, away from the curb. "Can you please lower the step?" I asked. "Step back," he directed.

I figured he didn't want my foot on the step while he lowered it. As soon as I stepped back, he closed the doors in my face and drove away. I was stunned. I choked back tears and waited for the next bus. He probably didn't realize that I had a disability, but I could have had a sprained ankle. Every time I walked to the bus stop, I prayed, *God, please let the bus come close to the curb or let it be a kneeling bus.* Sometimes I had to wait for two or three buses to get one that I could get on. When a bus stopped far from the curb, I'd look away and pretend that I wasn't waiting for the bus, or I'd glance down the block as though I were looking for someone. I was able to tell if the bus was going to pull in close to the curb by the way it was angled after it passed the traffic light. Leaving early was the best way to ensure I got to school on time since I had to be picky about buses. Most drivers on the kneeling buses would lower the step, so it was mostly the old buses that I needed to avoid. I was glad when there were older passengers getting on or off because I didn't have to ask the driver to lower it.

When I got to school, anxiety ensued as getting up the stairs was my next challenge. If my first class was on the third or fourth floor, I'd be afraid of being late. I tried to go up as fast as I could, but after a few steps, I'd run out of steam and lag behind. As I pulled myself up,

I arched my back. Once, a girl behind me yelled, "Stop putting your butt in my face." Others would suck their teeth or just go around me. There would be a large gap between me and the person in front of me and a backup of students waiting to run up, with me obstructing the staircase. I didn't want to bring attention to myself or make anyone uncomfortable, so I waited on the side for the others to pass as I did at Holy Cross, but it was different because I had several flights to climb, unlike my former school that only had one. If any stragglers entered the staircase, I would stop until they passed. Occasionally, a kind person would ask me if I was okay. I smiled and nodded.

One day, while Tina and I were walking through the campus with a friend, I fell. They kept walking for a few feet before they noticed that I wasn't with them. They turned and found me on the ground, then ran over to help me up. My jeans were torn open, and my knees were bleeding. Their kindness and concern brought tears to my eyes. I often got emotional when I fell. It hurt physically, and it was embarrassing, but it was the kindness that made me emotional. Each fall was a reality slap in the face. It was a reminder that this mysterious thing was still there. I sometimes felt that it was life's way of saying, "Don't try to be normal because you're not." At times like that I felt less than, broken, and disadvantaged. Tina put her arm around me as we walked through the campus. She then reached into her jacket pocket and handed me her elevator pass, "Here, you need it more than me." She was given the elevator pass for days when her asthma made climbing stairs difficult. "What will you do when you get asthma?" I asked. "Don't worry. I'll say I lost it, and they will give me another one," she said matter-of-factly.

The first time that I used her pass, I felt guilty. I worried that the elevator operator might ask for ID, compare the names, and then yell at me to get off the elevator. After a few weeks, though, I didn't even have to show it, but I always kept it with me just in case.

I told Tina that I loved having the elevator pass. She said, "When your mother first told me that you were walking slow and falling for attention, I believed her. But I know you aren't making it up, and I'm glad I could help you."

During my first semester at FDR, someone got the bright idea to make physical education coed. We met in the boys' gym, and after a couple of days of seeing what I was expected to do—in the presence of boys—I never went back. I failed that semester. A friend told me about a class called Disco Dance, taught by one of the deans, Mr. Gang. I loved it because we didn't have to change our clothes or sit on the floor. I was able to do the line dances and some of the partner dances without tiring. It was a popular class, so students were only allowed to take it once. Mr. Gang bent the rules for me and let me take it twice. One of the graduation requirements was to pass seven physical education classes, but I only had two P.E. credits.

I had no choice but to take regular P.E again. I was glad that it wasn't coed, but that didn't make it any easier. The girls' gym was on the second floor, and the locker room on the first. I felt anxious just thinking about getting dressed downstairs and walking up the flight of stairs. I opened the combination lock and removed my red shorts trimmed with white piping, my white T-shirt with the red letters *FDR*, and my sneakers. Since I couldn't take the elevator from the locker room, I had to make that strenuous climb. I pulled myself up the long narrow staircase, again waiting for the other girls to go up before me so I wouldn't block them from running up quickly.

The next horror was sitting on the floor spots. I tried standing on my spot when everyone in the class was sitting. I hoped that the teacher would not notice or care that I was standing. But of course, she would notice me right away, sticking out like a sore thumb. I felt stupid standing there when everyone was sitting, but looking stupid was better than sitting on the floor and not being able to get up. When the teacher told me to sit down, my heart started to pound in my chest like it was going to explode. I wished she would just let me stand there. I wanted to say, *No, I don't want to sit; I want to stand because it's hard for me to get up*. But of course, I couldn't say that. She would just ask me why and I wouldn't have an answer. Then she'd call Mom and hear that I was lazy or looking for attention. As soon as I was seated, I started to stress about how I would get up. I began to pray; *God, please help me. Help me get up*. My mind began to race. I looked at the girls around me. The one behind me looked nice.

"Hi, I hurt my leg; do you think you could help me up when it's time to get up?"

"Okay," she agreed and smiled at me.

Every day, she helped me up off the floor. When she was absent, I would look for someone else to help me.

I didn't mind the beginning of the semester so much. The teachers usually started us with stretching and floor exercises, which were easy for me. They had us do some drills that would later be used for the games we would be playing. Running up and down the gym dribbling a basketball was out of my realm of abilities. If volleyball was the sport, I could stand near the net and try to serve the ball but there was no way I was going to be able to run after a ball to hit it. When the activities got too difficult, I'd try to hide. It isn't easy hiding in an open gym, so I tried to pretend that I was doing what I was supposed to do. I watched the other girls in the gym. They chatted and giggled with each other like they had no worries. I envied them. Even the ones that weren't good at sports were able to do what I never could.

There was a girl in my class who never participated. She didn't even change into her uniform and try. I admired her for being a rebel. I wished I had the nerve to stand in defiance, wearing my regular clothes like she did. When it came time for the full-blown games of volleyball, basketball, or whatever sport it was for that quarter, I started standing on the side with her.

"So, you must hate coming to gym, too," I said. She smiled and nodded.

"Why don't you participate? I asked.

"I'm medically excused from P.E.," she said.

"I didn't know you could get medically excused. How did you get medically excused?" I asked desperately.

"I got a doctor's note because I have a back problem."

I became so thrilled about the possibility of getting out of gym class that I could think of nothing else. I needed to get a doctor's note, but I wondered how. I couldn't ask my mother; she would never go for that. I needed help from someone else.

Mary was eighteen years old and was working at the time. When I got home from school, I eagerly waited for her to get home from work.

"Hi. Guess what I found out today?" I blurted out as she entered our bedroom.

"What?" she asked as she put her bag down and stretched across her bed.

"You can be medically excused from gym."

"Really?" she asked.

"Yes. There's a girl in my class who said she's medically excused and she only needed a doctor's note to get it. I can't run and jump and do the stuff they want me to do in gym. If I don't pass, I won't be able to graduate. I can't ask Mommy, because she will tell the doctor I'm making it up. I need to find a doctor and I need money to pay for it."

"I'll help you pay for the doctor, but what doctor will you go to?" she asked.

"I don't know. I'll ask someone if they know of a doctor I could go to," I replied.

A year earlier, I had fallen while walking into the kitchen to put a plate in the sink. The plate broke and Dad rushed over to pick me up. "Something is wrong with this kid! She's always falling. You should take her to the doctor!" Wow! Finally! Until then, Dad was silent and never tried to find out what was going on with me. "Okay, I'll take you to a doctor to stop this once and for all," Mom said. She was going to prove me wrong, and I was hoping to prove her wrong.

The day of the appointment came, and after a short bus ride, Mom and I walked in silence toward the doctor's office that was on the first floor of an old Victorian house. The magnolia trees were in full bloom and the only sound was that of the chirping of birds on the quiet residential street of Glenwood Road. I was so excited to finally find out what was wrong with me. I couldn't wait to tell the doctor about my physical limitations and get cured. I hadn't been to a doctor since I was a young kid. This time, I would be able to explain my symptoms myself.

The doctor called me into the exam room and asked me to sit on the examination table. I sat on the crisp white paper that crinkled as I shifted my weight.

"So, why are you here?" he asked.

"I fall a lot and when I do, I can't get up without holding onto something. It's hard for me to go up the stairs. I need to use the railing to pull myself up, and I can't run. When I walk a lot, I get tired, and my muscles hurt."

He looked at me puzzled. The examination consisted of him squeezing my arms and legs. He used a reflex hammer to test my reflexes, but my reflexes were absent. After the exam, he and my mom walked into another room. I could see them talking through a glass window that separated us. I wondered what they were talking about. Soon, he returned and said, "I can't find anything wrong with you." I just sat there feeling helpless. I didn't know what to say. Looking back, I often wondered why these doctors didn't run any tests or think to refer me to a specialist. Maybe they did, but I wasn't privy to the conversations the adults were having.

My heart sank as my quest for truth was quashed. I thought that Mom had sabotaged my chance at finding out what was wrong with me. I was so heartbroken that I didn't speak to her all the way home. After getting off the bus, we walked down the block to our apartment building. She finally broke the silence.

"Are you satisfied? Are you finally going to stop insisting that something is wrong with you?" I couldn't believe her. I couldn't believe that she was actually saying that. "I heard you whispering to the doctor. I know that you told him that I am just making it all up for attention. I don't know why you tell everyone that I am making it up. It isn't true. I don't want to be like this. I want to be like everyone else. I don't like to fall; it's embarrassing."

She had no response. She did not deny my accusations. She put her head down and kept on walking. I was so disgusted that I didn't want to walk with her. I began to mince down the block in hopes that she would walk ahead of me like she always did. I wished for the large distances that separated us when I walked too slowly for her when I was younger. I wanted her to leave. I didn't want her to see the tears that I was fighting so hard to keep back. At that moment, I felt so helpless, so under her control, so beaten, so robbed of my truth, forced to live with a lie—a lie that was hers, not mine. She would rather view me as a liar than help me. She would rather have others believe that I am crazy than to believe that there is something wrong with me. Eventually, she picked up her pace. As she passed me, I allowed my tears to flow.

When I got home, I went into my room and sat on my bed. I didn't understand why she couldn't consider that maybe I was telling the truth. *Why was she acting this way? How could she be so blind? She was the smartest person I knew.* I tried to consider her theory. *Could she be right, and I am wrong? She is usually right. Maybe she's right. Maybe if I tried harder, I could be normal.*

I started to think that maybe I could overcome it with my mind. I thought that if I concentrated long enough, maybe I could use the mind-over-matter technique. I slid off my bed and got on the floor. I concentrated on my leg muscles as I told myself that I could do it. I wanted to believe that I was strong enough to overcome this weakness. I focused and tried to use willpower. I prayed to God to help me, but my muscles did not cooperate. It was like I was paralyzed. My legs ignored my plea and defied me. I slammed my fists against my thighs in frustration as I commanded them to rise. *Get up! Just get up, you can do it!*

I told myself. They did not obey my direction. *I hate you; I hate you*; I told them as I cried. I crawled over to my bed in defeat and surrendered, pulling myself up with my arms.

I got the name and address of a friend's physician. This time I would be going to a doctor that Mom had never met. I was scared and nervous. I didn't know what to expect. I was so used to doctors who didn't help me. When the doctor called me into the examination room, I entered with Mary.

"How can I help you?" he asked.

"I have problems walking and climbing stairs, and I fall a lot. I need a medical excuse from gym class."

"How long has this been happening?"

"It's been happening ever since I could remember."

"Where is your mother?"

"Our mother doesn't believe her, but she isn't making it up," Mary chimed in.

I almost died inside. I knew that she was trying to help me, but I didn't want her to even mention that someone didn't believe me, let alone my own mother. I knew he wouldn't take me seriously after that. He would think that I was a fraud and a cheat, trying to get out of P.E. I was devastated. The doctor just gave me the usual exam—touched my legs and asked me to walk. He did try to check my reflexes, but as usual, they were absent. I remember that he used two of those reflex hammers, one larger than the other.

"I can't write a note, because I don't know what's causing the symptoms that you are describing." My eyes welled up. I tried not to blink because that would send tears spewing.

"I can't do gym, and if I don't pass, I won't be able to graduate," I said as a final plea.

He must have seen the desperation on my face. He sat at his desk.

"I can only describe what you have reported to me," he stated as he began to write.

To whom it may concern:
L. A. has been seen at my office.
She is complaining of weakness and pain in her legs.
She is requesting to be excused from physical education class.

After reading the note, my heart sank to yet another level. I thought the note would never hold up, and the teacher would laugh at me and throw it in my face, saying, "Get downstairs and get prepared for class," or "There's nothing wrong with you. If everyone else can do it, so can you."

Nonetheless, I went to school with the note and a prayer. I prayed the night before and all the way to school, *God, please let her accept this note. Please take this hardship from me.* When I got to class, I walked over to her while she was taking attendance. She was a petite woman with short black hair. Her legs and arms were thin, and the skin on them was wrinkled and starting to sag. She wasn't very friendly and never seemed concerned about why I didn't participate. I patiently stood beside her until she finished. I was hoping that my body language would not give away the fear that I was feeling. If I looked too nervous, she might realize that the note was not good enough. My heart pounded and my hands trembled. I stood next to her as she read the note. It felt like she was taking too long to read it. I wondered if she was reading it twice because she didn't see the part that was supposed to say that I *should* be excused from gym, not, "She is *requesting* to be excused from physical education."

After what felt like an eternity, she turned to me and simply said, "Okay," then tucked the note in the back of her attendance book. I was pleasantly surprised and said, "That's it?" She said, "Yes," and that was the end of gym class for me. It was my "Get out of jail free" card. I went to class a couple of times after that but then stopped going altogether. I didn't see the point of standing there off to the side, not doing anything; besides, they couldn't fail me. I told the other girl who was excused that I wasn't coming back. I spent that period in the library doing homework.

At the end of the marking period, I handed my report card to Mom and went into my room across the hall. I anxiously waited for the moment when she noticed the letter "M" in place of a numeral grade for physical education. I imagined she would quickly turn the report card over reading the legend searching for what M stood for. Within a few seconds she yelled out.

"How did you get a medical excuse from gym?"

"I got a doctor's note," I yelled from my room.

I must admit there was smugness in my voice as I proudly answered with a grin on my face. She walked across the hall and stood in the doorway of our room.

"How did you get a doctor's note?" she inquired.

"Mary went with me to a doctor, and he gave me the note," I explained.

"You went behind my back to some quack?" Mom yelled.

"I can't believe you were part of this," she scolded Mary.

It was a little unpleasant for a few minutes to hear her yell, but it was worth it. High school became bearable as I no longer felt like an outcast who struggled in stairwells or an outsider who sat on the side in gym class. With the help of my sister and friend, I made it to graduation day.

Chapter 3

Diagnosis and Denial

After high school, Mom brought me to a job agency in Manhattan where her cousin worked. He helped me get my first job as a proofreader in the billing department of a maintenance corporation located at Two Penn Plaza, directly above Madison Square Garden. I was excited to work in the city. We lived near the F train, which was elevated. This meant that I had to walk one block and one long avenue to get to the station. Then, I had the arduous task of climbing three flights of stairs to get to the platform.

The thunderous sound of the trains overhead set off my anxiety as I walked toward the Ditmas Avenue station. I watched people rush by me, some running toward the stairs in hopes of getting to the top before the doors chimed, "ding dong," and closed in their faces. I tried to leave early because rushing wasn't an option. When my muscles were achy from the walk or stiff from the cold winter air, I walked even slower. I carried a sense of anguish as I approached the staircase. It was my Mt. Everest, and I needed to conquer it daily. Once I got to the stairs, I held on to the banister and rested before ascending. The staircase was sheltered by the one above it. The steps were concrete with metal tips on them. Some were speckled with black spots of discarded gum. The dirty yellow banister was my lifeline as I clutched it and pulled myself up each step, one by one. I had to be careful where I held on. Experience taught me that people on the platform spit down, and it sometimes landed on the railing. I also learned that it was another popular place for used gum. I rested in intervals, trying not to draw attention to myself. I looked out toward the street at the people hastily walking toward the station, pretending that I was looking for someone. I evaded eye contact so that no one would ask me what was wrong or if I was okay.

If someone did ask if I was alright, I had no explanation to offer them, and there wasn't anything they could do to help me. The only response I could give them was a smile and a nod. I hoped that they would run ahead of me and get on the train without noticing me. Although I wished to be unseen, the reverse would occur. Sometimes passengers getting off a train were coming down on one side of the staircase while I sluggishly climbed or rested on the other side, which made it impossible for others to pass me. I stood up against the railing, trying to make room for them to squeeze by. Occasionally, the sucking of teeth and snide remarks demonstrated their annoyance as I obstructed their path. New Yorkers are always in a rush and probably couldn't imagine why I was standing there or moving so slowly when there was a train to catch.

Once I conquered the first two flights, there was one final flight that led to the platform. I relished the fact that I could rest before the train came. If I made it up just before the train pulled out, a thoughtful person would sometimes stop and hold the door for me. The onlooking passengers were waiting for me to rush in so the doors could close, and they could be on their way. By then, I was too exhausted to hurry and would wave them on, saying, "No, thank you. You can let it go." I was too late for that train but early for the next.

As I waited behind the thick yellow line painted on the edge of the platform, I looked down the tracks to see if I could get a glimpse of the next train. With the worst part of my day behind me, I enjoyed a sense of accomplishment. In the warm weather, I soaked up the sunshine and enjoyed the warm breeze. If it was raining or cold, I huddled close to the wall under the awning. As I waited for the train, I could see a new set of commuters just coming up the stairs. They didn't see how I struggled to get up there. I felt normal in their eyes. They were the ones I didn't have to be invisible to.

If I didn't get a seat on the train, I held onto the pole tightly because the fast-moving train would jerk me around, threatening to knock me to the floor. If I did get a seat, I'd start worrying as I neared the end of my journey. I envied others that popped up out of their seats the moment the train stopped. Some were engrossed in the newspaper or magazine they were reading and were still able to jump up and hop over to the doors seconds before they closed. I had to get up the stop before my destination to ensure I had enough time to pull myself up out of the low seat and make my way to the doors before they closed. I'd rather get there too early than risk missing my stop.

I took the F train to 34th Street, then walked to the escalator near Gimbel's Department Store. Sometimes, as I followed the moving crowd, I'd find myself in front of an out-of-service escalator. The escalator steps were so steep that I had to turn away and find a staircase to climb. Once I was out on the street, I found it difficult to keep up with the quick, moving crowds. Like a scene in a movie, I walked in slow motion while a mob of commuters rushed past me. I felt like an alien who didn't belong in this fast-paced world. I was fearful of getting knocked down and learned to walk close to the buildings where fewer people passed. I would pretend to window-shop as an excuse to rest.

Once I arrived at work, I was as normal as anyone else, and no one knew the hardship I endured to get there. Going home was easier, because gravity made going down the stairs less difficult. If I held on to the banister and watched my step, I could descend quickly. I enjoyed working and was proud to be holding down a job. Although the stairs were a thorn in my side, I had become inured to struggling and never thought of quitting.

I turned eighteen on a cold, snowy day in early December. I put on a new pair of black velvet jeans and a white sweater. I was looking forward to celebrating my first day as an adult by going out to lunch with my coworkers Laura and Susan. When I stepped outside, the snow felt like white confetti cascading down upon me in celebration. The pure flakes fell steadily, beautifying everything. The dingy city was turned into an immaculate locale. Cars were blanketed in white, masking their true colors. The dreary gray concrete appeared clean and fresh. Snow outlined tree limbs, revealing majestic forms. A sense of tranquility filled the atmosphere. I crossed the street and began walking down the long avenue toward the train. A quarter of the way down the block, I slipped. My knees hit the ground like heavy sacks of coal, contrasting against the white ground. Before I could think about how I was going to get up, a stranger was behind me, lifting me off the ground. He lived in one of the old houses on the block that were sandwiched between apartment buildings. I had seen him before on route to the train. He was tall and handsome, with dark hair and blue eyes. He appeared to be in his late twenties. After picking me up, he examined me and asked, "Are you okay?" I nodded yes and looked down at my knees. My brand-new pants were torn open. I couldn't go to work that way, but I knew going home would make me late.

I asked the stranger, "What should I do? Should I go home?" He looked at me with concern and said, "Yes, I would go back." I smiled at him with watery eyes, said thanks, then turned around and headed home. I called out sick, took off my clothes, and got back into bed. I didn't want to be late, and the threat of falling in the slippery snow persisted. I cried into my pillow. I cried because I was disappointed to miss the festivities at work. I cried because my new pants were ruined. I cried because I knew there would be more pants destroyed and more gashes in my knees, but mostly because I didn't know why.

A couple of months after my birthday, a young man named Ricky got hired. All the girls in the office whispered about how handsome he was. He had the looks of a model, with dark hair and fine features. He was friendly and had a good sense of humor.

Ricky and I started dating after a couple of months of friendship. When he learned that I had never been to a sporting event, he took me to my first baseball game to watch the New York Yankees. He got tickets for us to see the Islanders play for the Stanley Cup (they won that day, and I had no idea how special it was). He brought me to a car show at the Jacob Javits Center and to Madison Square Garden to see the circus. When I mentioned that I loved the music from the fifties, he got us tickets to a doo-wop concert at MSG. We visited the top of the Empire State Building and enjoyed the breathtaking views of the city lit up at night. During the holiday season, we went to see the spectacular tree at Rockefeller Center. He brought me to the famous toy store FAO Schwartz and bought me a stuffed animal. Although I was a native New Yorker, I was discovering my city for the first time. When it came to my "condition," he was patient and understanding. He never rushed me or complained about my weakness. He walked slowly with me and rested with me when I was tired. I enjoyed experiencing new things with Ricky, and he enjoyed showing them to me.

My first year at the job was around the corner when Ricky came over to my desk. "What's a nice girl like you doing in a place like this?" he said.

Although I enjoyed working, I knew it wasn't a career job. I wasn't making much money and knew that I really didn't have the opportunity to move up. I had shared my dream of becoming a teacher with Ricky, and he was giving me a hint that maybe it was time.

I hadn't taken the SAT in high school, so I decided to start by getting my associate's degree at Kingsborough Community College (KCC). The college is in the Manhattan Beach area of Brooklyn, with a seventy-one-acre campus that overlooks Sheepshead Bay, Jamaica Bay, and the Atlantic Ocean. The cafeteria doors open onto the school's private beach. Many students joked that KCC stood for Kingsborough Country Club.

The first day of classes was March 1, 1982. I woke up to the sound of my parents arguing. When I got home from school, Dad was gone. I was nineteen years old; Megan was sixteen, and Mary was twenty-one. I knew that my parents had problems throughout their marriage. They even separated once for a couple of months. Mom was waiting to become financially independent before leaving him.

In September, Mary got married and moved out. With Dad and Mary gone and Mom working full time, everything changed. The family I had been part of no longer existed. The dinners and conversations at the dining room table were scarce. The era of watching television in the living room with Dad vanished. Although I was nineteen, I felt lost without Dad in the picture. I felt as though I had lost an ally.

School became my focus. I enjoyed attending classes. I felt empowered to make my dream of becoming a teacher come true. After obtaining my associate's degree, my plan was to transfer to Brooklyn College to pursue my bachelor's degree in teaching. While at Kingsborough, I ran for a position in student government. I became the treasurer of the Liberal Arts student council. As members of the student council, we planned trips to dude ranches and amusement parks for the students. We organized voter registration drives and sat on the board that decided how the student fees would be allocated. I had a lot of friends and enjoyed socializing. I went to parties, bars, and clubs with my friends. Mom didn't like me coming home late and expected me to follow the same rules she had established when I was fifteen: home by ten on weeknights and midnight on weekends. Clubs and discos didn't open until after ten O'clock. I'd have just enough time for one dance before I had to travel back home by midnight so, I broke the rules. This caused tension between us.

For the most part, my time at KCC was enjoyable. Most of the buildings had elevators, so the only challenge I had was getting on the bus and walking through the large campus to get to classes in different buildings. I tried to ignore my condition as much as possible. I didn't want it to stop me from accomplishing my goals and enjoying life, but it was always there, lurking in the shadows, reminding me that it was not going away. I tried to pretend that nothing was wrong. At times, I was afraid to have too much fun because life would inevitably knock me back down, reminding me that being "normal" wasn't a luxury I could enjoy. I was always aware of the challenge of stairs, but it was the unpredictable falls that crushed my spirit.

The worst fall at KCC happened on a stormy spring day. I was running late for biology class. Only two other people got off the bus with me, and the campus was deserted because of the inclement weather. The wind was powerful as it came off the ocean. I battled against it as I trudged toward the science building (the furthest building on campus). A twisted remnant of what had once been an umbrella rolled across the campus like tumbleweed. The open campus situated on a peninsula, had no structures to buffer the gusts. I felt like an autumn leaf desperately holding on in a windstorm. I lost my battle to stay erect when a squall brought me to my knees. As the rain beat down on me, the wind became my foe. Without a soul around to help me, panic set in. I looked up and saw a lamppost a few feet in front of me. I crawled on the hard, wet concrete toward it. I wrapped my arms around the cold, slippery pole and tried to pull myself up. After slipping off a couple of times, I finally got up and made my way to the building. Once inside, I was able to rest and warm up for a minute. After composing myself, I walked down the hall and entered the classroom. I apologized to my professor for being late and joined my classmates in examining fetal pigs.

It's scary to have no control, to be a hostage that has no say, imprisoned in a body that betrays you. I existed in two worlds, the normal and the abnormal. I did my best to hide the latter, but I would get caught impersonating the normal when my body failed me. It felt as if a spotlight was shown on me, revealing that I was an imposter.

Maybe Mom was right: I was a liar, a fake, and a fraud. But it wasn't the disabled world that I was a charlatan of.

Ricky decided to move back in with his parents to pursue a better job. Since they lived in New Jersey, we didn't see each other much. I began spending a lot of time in Tina and Lydia's apartment to fill the loneliness that I felt.

As I spent more time with the girls, I noticed that their brother Hector was home more frequently than before. Hector was two years older than me and very handsome. He inherited the chiseled bone structure of the native Taínos of Puerto Rico. He had big brown eyes and thick black hair that he wore in a pushed-back style, like James Dean. I remember passing his room once when I was fifteen. "Chantilly Lace" blared from his stereo. As I passed by, I peeked into his room and saw him looking in the mirror while combing his hair back. I thought he was cool, like the Fonz from the television show *Happy Days*. Although I thought he was incredibly handsome, he had a bad-boy vibe that intimidated me.

One night, on my way out, I passed his room as I did many times before. His door was open, and he called out, "Good night." I turned toward him and asked, "What are you doing home on a Saturday night?" He was rarely home when I hung out with his sisters.

"I've been drinking too much lately. I just finished a detox program at the hospital. I need to stay away from my friends because they are all still drinking. I need to stay away until I get stronger."

I was impressed with his honesty and surprised that he was sharing his personal struggles with me. Although I had been friends with his sisters for about five years by then, we had never had a real conversation before. We just said hello in passing. I thought that if it were me, I would be ashamed to admit to others that I had a drinking problem. I always tried to hide my problems and pretend that nothing bothered me. I was touched by his ability to disclose his weaknesses and flaws.

I got to know who was under the tough veneer, and I was moved by his vulnerability and honesty. As the weeks went on, Hector and I grew closer. He revealed how angry he was that his biological father left his mom and abandoned him and his sister. "If I ever saw my real father and my stepfather walking down the street, I would spit on my real father and hug my stepfather," he said.

During one of our talks, Hector disclosed that he wished he had never dropped out of school.

"You can get your high school equivalency diploma," I suggested

"I don't think I'll pass, because I missed so much," he confessed.

"You can do it; I'll help you study. All you need to do is get the GED practice book and sign up for the test."

"You really think I can do it?"

"Yes, of course I do."

We went to the library, checked out the preparation book for the test, and I started tutoring him. Math was his weakest subject; he needed the most help with algebra. I explained that it was like solving a set of puzzles, and as long as he knew the formulas, he would be able to solve the problems. Hector smiled with pleasure and enjoyed learning. He laughed in delight when he was able to solve the equations. After weeks of studying, he took the test and failed by three points. I encouraged him, "Retake it—that was a great score, considering that you barely went to school." He took the test again and was elated to find his high school diploma in the envelope with the passing scores. I was so proud of him, but more importantly, he was proud of himself, and it was just what he needed to build his self-esteem. As we got closer, I opened up to him and shared my feelings about my "condition." I felt like he understood what I was going through. He was like me in the sense that we both suffered from feelings of inadequacy. We bonded and formed a friendship.

There are so many falls that are embedded in my memory. I see myself in all ages and stages of my life on the ground. I can visualize myself

on the floor of rooms in different buildings and on the ground in different locations that I have fallen in. I envision the faces of family members, neighbors, friends, coworkers, and strangers as they picked me up off the ground. Of all the countless falls, there are a few that stand out as defining moments of my life.

One such fall occurred on my way to KCC. I was crossing the street to get change for the bus when I fell in the crosswalk. The traffic light flashed, warning that it was about to change, and the only thing separating me from a bus was a white painted line on the black asphalt. I was out in the open with nothing to hold onto. I couldn't get up. I felt stranded as I remained in the spot where I fell, frozen on my knees.

A silver-haired man in his fifties rushed over to pick me up and escorted me back onto the sidewalk. I was about to turn twenty years old and still had no idea what was happening to me. I felt like I had just been sucker-punched by an invisible opponent. Every fall was a punch in the face, and each punch was an attempt to keep me down. After the dozens of times that I had fallen, it never got easier, and it never stopped hurting emotionally.

The kind man asked me if I was alright. After assuring him that I was okay, I looked down at my torn jeans and bleeding knees. With blurred vision and trembling hands, I walked down the street back toward my apartment building. The raw skin on my knees burned as the rough cotton material rubbed against them.

I got into the elevator and put my finger on the silver button with the number two engraved in it. If I got off on the second floor, I wouldn't find comfort, but I knew that Nanny would be in her apartment and that she would tend to my wounds. I slid my finger to the button with the four on it. I rang her doorbell then heard her angelic voice call out, "Coming!"

When she opened the door, I greeted her with a quivering voice, "Hi, Nanny. Do you have any BAND-AIDs? I fell on the way to the bus stop."

"Sure, honey, come in," she said. I sat at her table, trying to stanch my tears while she gathered ointment and bandages. She gently and lovingly cleansed and bandaged my abrasions, then told me to go downstairs and change my pants.

"Here, take this and call a car service so you won't be late for class," she said as she slipped some money into my hand.

"Thanks, Nanny." As I kissed her goodbye, I saw a familiar look of sadness in her eyes. I was transformed into the eight-year-old child who once broke her heart by asking, "Nanny, what's wrong with my legs?" It was an unutterable question that continued to perplex me.

The next day, Nanny called and asked me to come up to her apartment. I figured she was going to ask me how my knees were healing.

"Come in, I have something to tell you." She closed the door and locked it behind me. Then she led me into her kitchen where a Chesterfield King cigarette with a long ash burned in an ashtray on the table. She spoke softly, as if someone might be able to hear her.

"I called your Aunt Colleen yesterday and asked her if she could find a doctor to help you find out what's wrong with your legs." I immediately became overwhelmed with excitement. "Don't let on to your mother about it. I don't want her getting mad at me," she warned.

"Don't worry, I won't tell her," I promised.

My Aunt Colleen made an appointment for me at the back clinic of the Hospital for Special Surgery. My cousin had scoliosis, and my aunt thought it would be good to start by checking my back. On the day of the appointment, Nanny, Nelly, my aunt, and I took a cab into Manhattan to the hospital. I was overjoyed that they were all supporting me. Nanny and Nelly chipped in for the hospital fee. I was ecstatic to be on the road to discovering what was causing my symptoms.

I went into the examination room alone while my team of supporters waited for me. The doctor listened carefully to my complaints. After a brief exam, he said, "I don't think that there's a problem with your back. A person of your age should not be having such difficulties. I'm going to refer you to the neurology clinic."

I was glad to see that I was being taken seriously. For the next appointment, Dad came with me. I entered the examination room smiling. The neurologist listened to my complaints with a serious look on his face. He tried to check my reflexes like all the other doctors before him. He did a basic muscle strength test. He started by asking me to squeeze his fingers then applied resistance against my muscles as I lifted my extremities in different positions. Then he examined my gait.

"I believe that you have a condition that is indeed very real, but I can't say for sure until testing is done to confirm. You will have to be admitted into the hospital for testing. You will need to have a muscle biopsy and an electromyography (EMG) test."

A nurse further explained, "For the muscle biopsy, they will make a small incision on the top of your thigh and take a small piece of muscle out to examine it under a microscope, For the EMG test, they will put small needles under your skin to examine how your muscles react to electric stimulation." I listened and nodded. I was willing to do anything to get answers.

"Do you have any questions?" the doctor asked.

"When will it be done? I have a break from school soon, but I'll be starting the spring semester at the end of February. Can it be done during the break, so I won't miss any classes?"

"We can arrange it in that timeframe," he assured me.

When I got home, I told Nanny what the doctor said, then added, "I'm going to have to tell Mom about the hospital stay and the surgery," She looked down, then nodded.

I didn't tell Mom until a couple of days before I was scheduled for the surgery. I was apprehensive about telling her because I was afraid of her reaction. I hoped that she would be supportive, but I had a feeling she would get upset, like she did when I got the doctor's note to get out of gym class. I finally mustered up the nerve to tell her. She was in her bedroom with the door closed. I knocked on her door.

"I have something to tell you. I'm going into the hospital for a couple of days."

"What hospital?" she asked as she opened her door and stepped into the small hallway that divided our bedrooms.

"The Hospital for Special Surgery. Nanny, Nelly, and Aunt Colleen took me there, and I'm going to have a muscle biopsy to find out what's wrong with my legs."

"You went behind my back with my mother and sister? Why do you keep insisting that something is wrong with you? There is nothing wrong with you! You just want something to be wrong with you so badly. They are going to make something wrong with you. They are going to cut you open like a guinea pig and experiment on you!"

"Well, if you really believe that I'm making it up, that means that I'm crazy. If I'm crazy, why don't you take me to a psychologist?"

"That's something for you to do," she answered.

I went into my room and closed the door. I couldn't understand why she thought my complaints, which spanned over two decades, were frivolous. We were able to speak of everything but my affliction. I thought that maybe she was holding onto her denial because she was afraid. Maybe she was afraid to admit that she had been wrong all these years, or maybe she was afraid that her daughter wasn't normal, and it was a reflection on her. Maybe she felt guilty that somehow it was her fault. I never faulted her, or anyone, for this nameless thing. I just wanted answers and to get better.

I sat on my bed and thought about the things I couldn't do, like going up the stairs easily, walking without fear of falling, running, and roller skating. I loved dancing and imagined myself dancing without stopping and resting before the song was over. I would be able to get up from a low chair without struggling and get up off the floor without a problem. I wouldn't have to stress out about buses and trains. I could move about the earth without anguish. I would prove to my mother that I wasn't making it up, and maybe she would say that she was sorry for not believing me. I would forgive her, and we would be close again.

I told my friends, and they were all excited for me. I had a friend named Jerry from school. He was happy for me. He said that he would buy me a bicycle and teach me how to ride it once I was better.

When I checked into the hospital, I was told that the Muscular Dystrophy Association (MDA) was sponsoring me and that I wouldn't be charged for any medical fees. During the first day of my stay at the hospital, I had the EMG testing. The next morning, I had the muscle biopsy. They used local anesthesia. I remember lying on the table in the cold, sterile room while bright lights shown down on me. The nurse prepped my thigh with a brown antiseptic, and the words that my mother yelled echoed in my head: "They are going to cut you open like a guinea pig and experiment on you!" For a moment, I wondered if she was right. What if this is a big mistake? I dismissed the negative thoughts and tried to focus on all the things I would be able to do once they found out what was wrong. I didn't feel pain, but I could feel pressure and pulling. After the incision was sewn, they dressed my wound and sent me back to my room.

Dad came to visit me with his new girlfriend, Judy. Ricky was unable to make the trip, but Hector came to see me. I wondered if mom would call or visit. I thought about the last time I had been hospitalized.

It was nine years earlier. Mom sent me and my sisters to a sleep-away camp. It was the first time we were away from home for an extended amount of time. We slept outdoors in tepees and covered wagons. We swam and skinny-dipped in the lake. We learned camp songs and sang them during meals in the large dining hall. We used latrines and cooked over outdoor fires. We boiled large pots of water to sterilize utensils.

One day, while boiling a large caldron of water, a girl in my group accidentally knocked it over, sending the scorching water rushing out and over my foot. I was taken to the infirmary, then later to a hospital, where I was told that I had third-degree burns.

My parents had decided to take a trip to Puerto Rico while we were away at camp. I was eleven years old and left in a hospital until my parents came back from their vacation. The days were long and boring. I thought about how my sisters were still at camp, having fun. Soon they would be going home, and I would be without my family for weeks.

One day, I looked up and saw my parents pass by my room. I was so happy and excited to see them. My mother had a worried look on her face. I was about to call out to them, but they walked into the room a few seconds later. Mom was carrying Leo the lion under her arm.

Leo was my favorite stuffed animal. He had green eyes and orange fur. He stood upright and wore boxing gloves. He had a banner across his chest that read, "Sock it to me." Seeing Mom come into that room with Leo under her arm brought me such joy. After seeing my parents and having Leo to comfort me, I knew everything would be okay.

Mom didn't visit or call me this time. Part of me knew that she wouldn't, but another part hoped that she would come through the door with a concerned look on her face and a stuffed animal under her arm.

A couple of days after the biopsy, I came home on crutches. Mom came into my room when she got home from work and asked, "How do you feel?" I smiled and said, "Okay." Nanny came down to our apartment, gave Megan some money, and said, "Make sure you help your sister."

Two weeks later, the bell rang. It was Dad. He was there to take me back to the hospital to have my stitches removed and find out the results of the tests. So far, it was the most exciting day of my life. I buzzed Dad in and stepped out into the hallway, limping, and said, "Hey look, no crutches!" Dad smiled as he walked up the stairs toward me. "Oh, that's great," he said. I locked the door, then we walked toward the elevator.

The drive to the hospital felt exceptionally long. I was full of hope and excitement. It was a cold, clear winter's day. As we drove along the FDR Drive, I watched a ship moving slowly across the East River. I wondered where it was going. I thought about my own voyage. I was on a journey to find truth, and there would be healing at the destination.

I was waiting excitedly in an examination room when the doctor entered. I couldn't contain myself and blurted out, "So, did you find out what's wrong with me?" He said, "Yes, but first, let's remove the stitches." He asked me to change into a gown so that they could remove the stitches from my thigh. After I changed back into my clothes, he returned with Dad and two women. One introduced herself as a psychologist and the other as a genetics counselor. I recall thinking that they all looked so serious. I was eager to hear the results and could not contain myself.

"So, what is it? What's wrong with me?" I thought it was strange that he wasn't smiling. After all, I was going to find out once and for all what was wrong with me.

"You have spinal muscular atrophy." It has a name, I thought. It is real. I had been validated. I was beaming while he spoke. He went on to say that it was a motor neuron disease.

"Okay, so, how can we fix it?" I asked ignorantly. He looked at me with sadness.

"Unfortunately, there is no known treatment or cure at his time. The disease is progressive—you will get weaker over time."

The question that broke Nanny's heart and scared my mother into denial was finally answered. The question that I stopped asking but never stopped wondering about was no longer a mystery. The devastating words of the doctor erased my smile and terminated my hopes and dreams of being normal.

The genetic counselor explained, "It is a recessive inherited disease. Both parents must be carriers, and when they both pass on the gene, the child gets the disease."

"Can you write the name down for me, so I won't forget?" I asked the doctor.

"Sure," he said, looking for a piece of paper. I watched him write the name down, then sat there staring at the words written in his small, crooked handwriting.

For much of my life, I had dreamed of this moment, imagining it as triumphant. I hadn't even considered the possibility of it not being treatable or curable. I never once considered that it was a lifetime sentence.

"Are you okay?" the psychologist asked, after observing my silence and changed expression.

"So that means that I'm always going to be falling and having a hard time climbing the stairs?" I asked.

"That's okay; when you get married your husband will buy you a ranch house," she responded.

"Get married? How could I get married and have kids?" I inquired.

"Lots of weak people have kids," she said, trying to reassure me that I will still be able to have a normal life.

The drive back into Brooklyn was very different; just hours before, I was filled with hope and excitement. As I peered out of the passenger window, I thought about how telling Nanny wasn't going to be the festive event that I thought it would be.

Soon, Dad and I were standing in front of Nanny's door. He rang her bell, then I heard her voice call out, "Coming." I listened to her feet shuffling toward the door, then the sound of the metal clicking as she unlocked it. A wave of sadness swept over me. I wished I had good news for her. Dad and I stepped into her apartment and sat at her table. Nanny had a serious look on her face, as if she knew it was going to be bad news.

"We found out what it is. It's called spinal muscular atrophy, but they said that there is no cure for it." I looked into her eyes searching for comfort. Her eyes were mirrors reflecting the sadness and disappointment that I was feeling. I reported that it was genetic and that I inherited a gene from each of my parents.

"No one on either side of my family ever had it," Nanny commented.

"No one in my family had it, either," Dad chimed in.

"Well, at least we know what it is," I said trying to be positive. We sat around for a few minutes, then Dad said he had to get going. We said goodbye to Nanny and left her apartment. Dad rode down in the elevator with me and walked me to the door. I kissed him goodbye and walked into the apartment. It was quiet and empty. There was no one to talk to; no one to comfort me.

I didn't tell Mom that day. I don't know why. Maybe I knew that she really didn't want to know, or maybe I couldn't handle another negative reaction from her.

That night, I went up to Nelly's apartment where she and Nanny were watching the news. I asked if I could use the phone to call Ricky. I became emotional when I heard him say hello.

"Hi. So, I found out what it is. It's called spinal muscular atrophy, but there's nothing they can do about it, and it will get worse over time." I tried to mask my trembling voice.

"It'll be okay; you could do exercises to keep the strength you do have." I knew he was trying to cheer me up, but nothing he could say would change the fact that I would never live a normal life. I wished that I didn't have to tell him on the telephone. I wished that he had come to see me and that he was there to hold me. Despite his positive words, I felt so alone. Tears streamed down my cheeks as I recalled him telling me that his mother would have something negative to say about me having something wrong with me. He mentioned that his sister's boyfriend had a brother with cerebral palsy, and his mom had commented that if she married him, their children could be defective. I knew his mother would never want him with an impaired person. Until then, it hadn't been a permanent affliction. I felt broken.

The next day, I went upstairs to see Tina, Lydia, and Hector. Lydia opened the door and led me into Hector's room, where they were all gathered. I sat on the end of the bed next to Tina. Hector was standing near his dresser, facing us, and Lydia was standing beside the bed.

"I found out what it is, but the doctor said there is nothing they can do about it. It's a neuromuscular disease, and they said it will get worse as I get older." They hung their heads in sadness. Lydia broke the silence with, "That's fucked up," shaking her head. I nodded and smiled nervously as I tried to hide my emotions. Lydia was right; it was simply fucked up.

A few weeks after my diagnosis, I was sitting at the dining room table. Mom's geraniums, with their pink flowers filled the windowsills. They stretched through the blinds toward the sun that flooded into the room from the two windows facing me. I was reading a pamphlet that I received from the Muscular Dystrophy Association about SMA. Reading it was such a validating experience. Everything that I had complained about was spelled out in front of me as if I had written it myself. I found it comforting.

The pamphlet informed me that there were different types of SMA. Werdnig-Hoffmann disease, or infantile, was characterized by onset at 0 to 6 months of age (today known as SMA1). Dubowitz, or intermediate, has an onset at 6 to 18 months (today known as SMA2). Kugelberg-Welander, or juvenile, has an onset at 12 months or later (today known as SMA3). I fell into the category of juvenile onset, or SMA3, because I walked and didn't show signs of onset until after 12 months. I also read that the ability to walk could end ten years after onset. I didn't know how long I had before it happened to me. I thought that I might be walking on borrowed time.

Mom was in the kitchen. I wanted her to read the pamphlet. I needed her to know, once and for all, that I was not making up my condition. There was something about the words printed in black letters against the white pages that made them seem official. The same words describing my symptoms were uttered by me but were never taken seriously by Mom. Maybe the written words would bring legitimacy to my complaints. My heart raced as I wondered how she would handle the information. I had to show her. I called her over and handed her the pamphlet. She took it in her hand and read the cover, which had **THE MUSCULAR DYSTROPHY ASSOCIATION** written vertically and **SPINAL MUSCULAR ATROPHY** written horizontally. After reading the title, she dropped the pamphlet on the table and walked away, saying, "I don't have time for this." For two decades, she had squelched my pleas for answers. She had robbed me of my truth and now of my exoneration. I didn't expect her to say that she was sorry for being wrong all those years, but I had hoped that she would at least read the information and say something like, *oh, so that's what was causing your weakness* or *I'm sorry that there isn't a treatment or cure*. Although she didn't read the pamphlet, the title alone gave her an idea of how serious the diagnosis was. Thanks to Jerry Lewis and the Labor Day telethon, we knew that muscular dystrophy was a serious, sometimes life-threatening disease. I had imagined the day that I could prove to Mom that my illness was real as a victorious day, but there were no winners on this day. My disability had been a silent but salient wedge between us for years. After my diagnosis, the wedge widened.

 Mom had always been strict, but with Dad no longer there to provide balance, she became unreasonable. If I stayed out past curfew, she'd lock me out of the house. I rebelled and would have to spend the night at a friend's house. Mom didn't like most of my friends. She forbad me from bringing Tina and Lydia into our apartment. She didn't want me going up to their apartment either, but again, I rebelled.

 I wanted to impress her with good grades because I thought it would make her proud of me as it did when I was a kid. I tried to show her my transcript. "Look, I got all As and Bs," I said proudly. Mom was in front of her dresser, looking in the mirror and combing her hair. Without looking at me, she silently nodded her head and kept combing. I didn't understand her behavior because I thought she would be pleased that I was doing what she always talked about—going to college to get an education.

Mom started making my life at home unbearable. She kept things like toothpaste, shampoo, and laundry detergent locked up in her room. If I asked for these items her response was, "Get a job."

"But I'm going to school," I explained.

"Lots of kids go to school and work," was her answer.

Lots of kids didn't have to struggle to get on the buses or trains, I thought. Kingsborough was two bus rides or one train and a bus away. I couldn't imagine traveling to yet another location.

When Megan wanted these necessary items, Mom would give her the amount she needed, then lock it back in her room.

"How come Megan gets to have some?"

"You are over eighteen years old. You are not my responsibility," Mom informed me.

I went up to Nanny's apartment with my toothbrush in my hand.

"Nanny, can I borrow some toothpaste? Mom keeps it locked up in her room and won't let me have any."

"I don't know where she gets that from. She doesn't get it from me," Nanny said shaking her head as she fetched the toothpaste. Eventually, I started asking dad for money for personal things.

One day, a friend at school approached me and asked, "Hey, why didn't you tell me that you moved?"

"What are you talking about? I didn't move." I said confused.

"Well, I called you last night, and your mother said that you don't live there anymore."

When I got home, I asked Mom, "Why are you telling my friends that I don't live here anymore?"

"I'm not your personal answering service," she answered. I began to feel like I was no longer a family member. I was a burden, and Mom didn't want me living with her.

The summer after my diagnosis, Lydia invited me to go with her and her parents to Coney Island Beach. It was a hot day, and I had nothing to do, so I happily agreed to go with them. When I got home, I went into my bedroom to get some clothes before taking a shower. Mom must have seen me getting out of the car with Lydia and her parents, because she stormed into my room yelling.

"I told you that I don't want you hanging around with those people from the sixth floor."

"I'm over eighteen. I'm not your responsibility," I answered flippantly.

"Get out," Mom yelled.

"Okay, let me get my clothes," I answered.

"No, get out now!" Mom demanded.

I was barefoot, wearing a pair of shorts and a halter bathing suit top. I insisted on getting some clothes and my shoes, but Mom refused to let me. She shoved me toward the doorway to push me out of my room. I fell on the floor and crawled toward a chair in the corner of my room. I was going to use it to pull myself up, but Mom followed me and grabbed me by my legs, dragging me toward the door. I clutched a leg of the chair, pulling it with me. When the chair blocked the doorway, she let go of my legs and pried my fingers free one by one, then held my hands so I wouldn't be able to reach for the chair legs. She then dragged me by my arms to the front door. The whole time I was screaming. "Get off me! I want to get my clothes!" I tried kicking to get free, but she was much stronger than me. She got the front door open and pulled me over the threshold and across the floor several feet to where the elevator was. She let go of my arms, leaving me on the cold, dirty stone floor, then stepped over me and ran back to the apartment, slammed the door shut, and locked it behind her. I crawled over to the staircase to pull myself up, then took the elevator up to

Tina and Lydia's apartment. Tina opened the door, and I fell into her arms, trembling and sobbing. She hugged me and brought me into her room. She and Lydia asked their mom if I could stay with them. Her mom, Angela allowed me to stay in her home, and I became part of their family.

Living with them eventually led to Hector and me being in a relationship. I broke things off with Ricky. I needed to be with someone that was emotionally available. I didn't want a long-distance relationship with someone who came around occasionally. I thought about his family, and I couldn't bear to be around people who looked down on me or didn't accept me. I knew there was no future with Ricky. I became committed to building a life with Hector and my surrogate family.

Chapter 4

Marriage, Motherhood, and Mayhem

The knowledge that I would lose my ability to walk gave me a sense of urgency, almost like a death sentence. I felt propelled into a game of "beat the clock" and knew I needed to change the course my life was on. I had always known I wanted to have children one day, but it had become my primary focus. The doctor's words—"It is progressive, and you will get weaker"—echoed in my mind. I planned to finish my associate's degree but decided not to pursue furthering my education. As Hector and I grew closer, I shared my desire to have a baby. A year later, we were planning to find our own apartment, get married, and start a family.

I had always had an unpredictable menstrual cycle, so I figured we should start sooner than later. I had skipped my period for seven months and thought I should see a doctor to help me become more regular. Hector went with me to the clinic. I was expecting to walk out with some pills to help regulate my cycle. I was shocked when the doctor examined me and said, "You are five weeks pregnant." I didn't know what to say, but I was immediately filled with joy. I walked over to Hector in the waiting room and said, "Let's get out of here." I was trying to control the elation plastered on my face. When we got outside, he asked me why I was smiling. I blurted out, "I'm pregnant. We are going to have a baby." Hector was surprised, but he smiled and hugged me. I couldn't believe that I had a tiny life growing inside me. I told Hector that we shouldn't tell anyone until we get married, but we told his sisters when we got home.

After the shock wore off, I began to worry about how SMA would affect my pregnancy. I made an appointment to see a neurologist. After I informed him of what SMA was (most doctors never heard of it, so I described it as a type of muscular dystrophy), he did a strength test and said that it wouldn't be easy to care for a baby. He then asked me if I wanted to continue the pregnancy. I emphatically answered, "Yes, of course I do!" He went on to say that I would need help from other family members. I wondered if the weight of the pregnancy would affect my walking, but he did not know. I thought I might need to use a wheelchair at the end when the weight was greatest. I weighed about a hundred pounds and couldn't imagine carrying extra weight, but I was willing to do whatever I needed to get through it.

By the end of the summer, I had completed all my requirements for my associate's degree and focused on my pregnancy and the start of a new chapter in my life. I read books about pregnancy and childbirth and shared the information with Hector. Together, we excitedly learned about the different stages of the baby's development.

On a warm October day in 1984, Hector and I got married in a civil ceremony. We took a cab to the courthouse with Lydia and Hector's best friend, Jr. I wore a cream-colored dress with light brown trim that fell right below the knee. Hector wore a black suit with a white shirt.

We had put some money down on a pair of wedding bands, but they wouldn't be sized by the time we were getting married. When my parents broke up, Dad gave me his wedding ring and Mom gave hers to Megan. I borrowed Mom's ring from Megan, and Hector used Dad's ring for the ceremony.

We took the train home, and while we were walking across the platform to exit the station, Hector saw a friend on the other side of the platform and yelled out "Hey, I just got married." As the train pulled into the station on the other side, I fell. I was so glad that the train was blocking us. How embarrassing for me to fall right after that public announcement of our marriage. Hector quickly picked me up. I scraped my knees and tore my stockings but smiled and pretended that it didn't hurt.

We arrived home to an empty apartment. There were no festivities planned. There weren't any congratulatory exclamations, cake, dinner, or gifts. But we didn't expect anything and were simply happy to be married. After hearing about our marriage, Nanny and Nelly gave us cards that each included one hundred dollars. I decided to save the money to pay for our rings once they were sized.

Hector was working as a security guard in an office building in the city. While he worked, I kept our room tidy and the laundry clean. I often sat in the kitchen and kept Angela company while she cooked family dinners. She wore a smile of contentment that reflected her love of cooking. I watched her every night and learned as I observed her.

Dad had married Judy, and they were expecting a baby in November. I was invited to her baby shower but only had the money I was saving for our rings. I decided to borrow a little of it to buy a gift. However, when I looked in the drawer where I kept the money, it was all gone. I asked Hector why he had taken it. He said he had lost his job and didn't want to tell me, so he borrowed the money to use for carfare. I suspected he used the money to get high. When I confronted him about it, he didn't deny my accusations. I realized that he must have been dipping into the money for a while to buy pot and beer. An argument ensued between us. He went into the kitchen, spoke with his mother, and then stormed out.

Angela came into the room and yelled at me in Spanish. She said that if I wanted a rich man, I should not have married her son. Based on what she was saying, I figured Hector must have told her we were fighting because I wanted money for the baby shower gift, and he didn't have it. He conveniently left out the part that he took the money and used it to get high. After she finished scolding me, I wrote a letter explaining what had happened. I put the letter on Lydia's dresser and left.

With nowhere to go, I went to Nanny's apartment and asked her if I could use her phone. I called my sister Mary and asked her if I could stay with her for a day or two, then asked Nanny for money for car service. While I was waiting, I heard a knock on the door—it was Lydia. She was holding my letter in her hand. With watery eyes, she told me that she read the letter to her mom. She wanted me to go back upstairs so she could apologize. I told her I was waiting for a cab and would talk another time. I spent a night or two with my sister but, I was ashamed to tell her what happened.

When I returned to the neighborhood, I heard someone calling my name. It was Hector. He came running over toward me, hugged me, and apologized. He told me that he had found a job with a construction company. He promised to do better and said he would get our rings out of the shop. A week later, he came home with our rings. He placed mine on my finger and professed his love for me.

In December, Hector and I found out that there was a vacancy for rent in the building. It was a three-room apartment on the first floor, which would be great for me in case the elevator wasn't working. The super let us look at it. As we stepped in, we entered a long hallway that ran the length of the apartment. On the right was a large living room with two windows facing the back courtyard of the building. Halfway down the hallway, also on the right was a small galley kitchen, preceded by the bathroom. At the end of the hallway, we reached the bedroom. It also had two windows facing the back. There was a closet next to the door on the right. I scanned the room and decided that the bed would go against the largest wall, facing the door, and a crib would fit nicely in the corner of the adjacent wall.

We didn't have enough money saved up for the apartment so, I asked Nanny if she could help us. She and Nelly gave us the money for the first month's rent and the security deposit. We let the super know that we were interested in the apartment, and the landlord agreed to let us rent it. The lease would start after New Year's Day at $373 dollars a month. We were so happy to have a place of our own to raise our baby.

When we were finally given the keys to our new apartment, I went in with Lydia to clean the place. The electricity hadn't been turned on yet because we needed a copy of the lease to get an account with the power company. I tried to clean during daylight hours. Hector and I were so anxious to start living in our new home that we decided to move in without electricity while we waited for the lease to be mailed to us.

The showerhead in the bathroom was missing, so on our first night in our new apartment, we filled the tub and lit candles around the room. Hector helped me into the bathtub and sat behind me. As I lay against his chest, he caressed my belly while the flickering light cast dancing shadows on the walls. The warm water surrounded us like a blanket. We were content to be settling into our own apartment. It was great having our own place to make a home.

By February, I had saved a hundred dollars toward a crib and was excited about getting everything ready for the baby, who was due on the twenty-fourth. A couple of weeks before my due date, I bumped into Nanny in the elevator. I smiled and said hello, but she ignored me.

"What's wrong? Why aren't you talking to me?" I asked.

"Hector asked me if he could borrow money for the first month's rent. He said he started a new job and was waiting to get paid, but he never paid me back," she informed me.

I had no clue that he had gone to her and borrowed money. I had been under the impression that he paid the rent. I felt so bad that Nanny was angry with me. I went into my apartment and got the money that I was saving for the crib, and brought it up to Nelly's apartment.

"I didn't know about your deal with Hector, and I shouldn't be punished for him failing to honor your agreement." Nanny and Nelly were silent while I spoke.

"Here is the money I've been saving for a crib; it's all I have." I placed the money on an end table and left the apartment. The next day, Nanny showed up at my door with some food from a restaurant. It was her way of saying that she was sorry. She never mentioned the money again.

I asked Hector why he borrowed money from Nanny. He said he lost his job but didn't want me to worry, so he went out every day looking and finally found another job with a moving company. He assured me that there was nothing to worry about, and I believed him.

It had been over a year since Mom threw me out. We had only crossed paths once, a few months afterward. I was in the elevator when it stopped on the fourth floor. When the door opened, I was shocked to be face-to-face with her. She seemed surprised as well. She said, "Oh," then let the door close and walked toward the stairs.

Since Mom and Dad broke up, much had changed. Shortly after Mary got married, she had a daughter, who was now already two years old. Like Dad, Mom had remarried and was expecting a baby boy in December.

After my brother was born, Megan told me that Mom felt bad that I hadn't seen the baby and coaxed me into visiting her. It felt strange walking into the apartment that had once been my home with Mom, Dad, and my two sisters.

I waddled into my mother's room with my huge belly preceding me. Mom greeted me with a smile. My brother had a sweet little face and a long body with thin, wrinkled legs. Mom was happy to show off her son. She asked me when I was due and said that she dreamed that I had a girl. She informed me that Nanny and Nelly had asked her to pick out a crib for me and that they would give it to me after I gave birth. I didn't stay long, but the meeting was pleasant, and it marked the end of our feud.

My pregnancy hadn't prohibited me from doing anything that I could do before. It was a little harder to climb stairs and walk, and I only fell once on my knees, but I didn't get hurt, and neither did the baby. I ended up never needing a wheelchair and was proud that I was able to get through the pregnancy without SMA complicating it.

On the evening of February 28, four days after my due date, I went into labor. Hector took me to the hospital. When the doctor examined me, I heard a nurse ask if I was having twins because my belly was so big. I informed her, "I had an ultrasound; there's only one baby." After many hours of labor, Hector said, "She can't do it." I knew he was thinking that SMA was the reason. "That has nothing to do with it," I snapped. The doctor decided that a C-section was needed because of the size of the baby. I was given general anesthesia and quickly fell asleep. On March 1, 1985, at the cusp of winter with spring on the horizon, I heard a nurse calling my name. I opened my eyes and heard her say the most beautiful words that had ever been spoken, "You had a baby boy. He weighs nine pounds and one ounce." I smiled and felt a tear run down my cheek, then closed my eyes and fell back to sleep. It had been my greatest accomplishment and my proudest moment.

Christopher was the biggest baby born that day. He was talked about by all the nurses. I recall my dad saying, "That's my grandson; he is going to be a football player." Mom came to visit me with Aunt Colleen. She told me that she would set up the crib that Nanny and Nelly had purchased before I got home.

I didn't get to hold or see my son for a few days because I was running a fever. I was too weak to get up and walk down the hall to the nursery to see him. I relied on family members to tell me how he looked. A couple of days later a nurse came in saying, "Get up! Get up! It's time to get out of bed," as she pulled the curtain to the side.

"I can't," I told her.

"The other mothers are getting up and walking."

"I'm not like other mothers. You should read my chart because I have a form of muscular dystrophy," I informed her.

Her eyes widened as she was taken aback by my statement. The next day she returned and helped me out of bed and into a chair. I just needed a little more time to heal and get my strength back.

I complained about not seeing my baby yet, so a nurse brought him to my bedside. She opened the blanket that he was wrapped in and turned him around so I could get a good look at him from every angle. He was absolutely perfect. Before I knew it, she rushed him out of the room. My heart ached to hold him. After my fever subsided, I was allowed to hold and feed my baby. I stared at my precious child. I was in awe of the new life that lay helplessly in my arms. I felt blessed to be given the opportunity to fulfill this dream called motherhood. I took delight in inhaling that newborn smell from his tiny head. His cheeks were chubby and rosy. I caressed his incredibly soft, fair skin. He was beautiful, and he was mine. As he lay heavy in my arms, I hoped I'd be able to carry him. I tried to put the unknown out of my mind. I told myself that I would figure it out. I'd learn how to care for him and how to prevent SMA from tarnishing my dream. I couldn't wait to get him home, bond with him, and enjoy being a family.

Tina came to the hospital with Hector to pick me up. We watched as the nurses dressed Christopher and swaddled him in a blue blanket. One of the nurses escorted me out to the front of the hospital in a wheelchair, which was standard practice, to a waiting car service. Tina carried the baby to the car and handed him to me once I was seated. When we got home, Hector carried the bags, and she carried our precious bundle into the apartment for me so I could hold onto the banister while going up the stairs.

When I walked into the bedroom, I saw the crib in the corner. Mom purchased the crib bedding set and had it all put together for the arrival of our son. She also got us a highchair, even though the baby wouldn't be able to use it for a few months. Dad bought us a dresser/changing table and had it delivered to the apartment.

I asked Tina to put the baby in the crib while I put our things away. As soon as I finished, Christopher began to fuss a little. "He's probably hungry," she said. I felt nervous about picking him up in front of her. *What if I can't? What if I struggle?* I wondered. "Do you want to feed him?" I asked. She quickly agreed. I handed her one of the bottles that the nurse sent us home with. I couldn't wait to be alone so that I could figure out how to lift him up and carry him in private. For the next feeding, I was alone. I lifted him up, then leaned my arms on the side of the crib railing, then lifted him higher. I practiced lifting him out and onto the changing table, being very careful and mindful of every movement and every step I took. Although it was a little bit of a struggle, I felt confident after doing it a few times.

In the next few days, family and friends visited and brought gifts as they shared in our joy. It was such an exciting and happy time for me. I knew motherhood would present challenges, but I was ready to meet each and every one of them. Mom gave me a rattan rocking chair. I used it to rock Christopher to sleep. Once he was asleep, I continued to hold him for a while longer. I stared at him in awe and watched him as he slept in my arms. I was overwhelmed with pride and love for this tiny life that we had created together. When it was time to transfer him to the crib, I couldn't stand up with him in my arms, so I called Hector. He would take him from me and gently place him in his crib. If Hector wasn't home, I would make sure that the rocking chair was very close to the bed. Once the baby fell asleep, I placed him on the bed, then used my arms to get up out of the chair. Once I was standing, I could pick him up and place him in the crib.

We didn't have a washing machine of our own, so we washed our clothes up in my mother-in-law's apartment. Hector asked his mom to come down and help me bring our laundry up to her apartment. Angela came down and carried the laundry bag while I carried the baby. I carried him from his crib, down the long hallway of the apartment, and then down the hall of the building to the elevator. As we waited for the elevator to come, he got heavier and heavier in my arms.

While we were going up in the elevator, the weight of the baby was too much for my arms to bear. I was struggling to hold him and was fearful that my arms would give out. I anxiously asked her to take the baby from me. She saw me struggling to hold him and said, *"Necesitas aprender."* ("You need to learn.") It wasn't as simple as learning how to carry him. I just didn't have the strength. I realized that I was limited in how long I could carry him. After that experience, I learned that I could not trust my arms. I could carry him from one room to another, but I never carried him outside the apartment again. I wouldn't have the strength to last more than a few feet, but more importantly, I was fearful of falling while carrying him. Even if I managed to keep him in my arms, I wouldn't be able to get up. After that day, I used the infant seat to carry him around. It was heavier to carry him in it, but it had a handle, and I could set it down if my arms got tired. As the baby grew and got heavier, I got a stroller, which made life much easier. When I needed to put him in the stroller, I brought the stroller next to the crib, so I didn't have to carry him too far. One time I lifted him up and out of the crib while he was sleeping and when I turned to put him in the stroller, I fell on my knees. He was still in my arms and didn't wake up. I placed him on my bed, then pulled myself up. Once I was standing, I transferred him from the bed to the stroller. I was so thankful that I didn't drop him.

I found ways to do other chores, like sterilizing bottles. Back then, we sterilized them in a big pot of boiling water. I had Hector fill the pot and place it on the stove before he went to work. After boiling the bottles, I removed each one from the pot using a large serving fork. I enjoyed making the bottles. I felt accomplished as I admired how they looked lined up in the refrigerator.

I continued to learn how to get around the effects of SMA. As the baby got bigger, it was difficult for me to lift him out of the crib. Once he learned how to sit, things got easier. I would turn him around with his back facing me. Next, I'd wrap my arms around his body and pull him up then rest him in a sitting position on the railing of the crib.

Then he was high enough for me to lift him out of the crib. Once he was in my arms at a good height, I could carry him a few feet to the kitchen to put him in the highchair. I was able to get him into the swing, but I couldn't get him out because of the angle. I didn't use the swing unless someone was around to help me get him out. Bathing wasn't bad because I put the infant tub on the kitchen counter, which was at a good height.

The older and more independent he got, the easier it was for me. When he was able to stand, he would stand up in the crib and put his arms around my neck. I placed my arms around him, and as I pulled him up, he would wrap his legs around me. As he got old enough to use the big tub, I placed a towel on the edge of it and held his hands to help him climb on the tub's edge. Then he would be high enough for me to lift. Once he started walking, things got even easier. He was very independent and wanted to do things on his own. He was a climber. He tried climbing into the stroller, highchair, and bath. Once I saw that he was initiating climbing into things, I let him. All I had to do was stand near him with my hands behind him for support in case he missed a step or slipped. I was proud that I was able to take care of my baby with little help from anyone. I was being a mom and not letting SMA get in the way.

My parents continued to be generous. Dad purchased a living room set for us. I promised to make the payments, but after I gave him the first one, he handed it back to me and said, "Keep it, but don't tell him." Mom bought us a used kitchen set that was in great condition. She also showed up at my door with a brand-new rug for the living room—items that I had not asked for. She knew that Christopher was crawling around on the hardwood floors and thought it would be easier on his knees. On our first Christmas as a family, the Christmas tree glowed in the corner of our newly decorated living room. Under it was an abundance of presents for our baby's first Christmas. I wanted to create good memories of Christmas mornings, like the ones I had growing up. I imagined coloring eggs with Christopher for Easter. I had plans for taking him to the parks, zoos, and beaches, like Dad did with us. I imagined him playing with a sibling one day and having memories of birthday parties, playing board games, or using their imaginations to create games of their own. There were so many joyful moments to come.

Hector had a new job installing windows for a window installation contractor. He was hired by the company after he asked if they needed help when they worked in our building. Hector was good with his hands and picked up the skill quickly. This job paid more than the moving company.

When Hector was home, he helped me with lifting and carrying bags when we went shopping. When he saw me struggling to vacuum, he would take the vacuum from me and say, "Sit down, I'll do it." If we went anywhere that had stairs, he picked me up and carried me. He'd flex his muscles and say, "That's what you have me for." We enjoyed watching our son grow and marveled at each new thing he achieved. SMA wasn't progressing. I was content to have a simple family life.

When my housework was done, I often went up to Angela's apartment and spent a few hours with her while Hector was working. I listened to her sing little songs in Spanish to the baby and enjoyed her delight when he interacted with her.

One day while I was visiting her, the phone rang. She handed me the phone and said, "It's for you." I was confused because I never received calls on her telephone. There was a woman on the other line.

"Are you Hector's wife?"

"Yes, who is this?"

"My husband and your husband are doing coke together. Your husband is fucking around with a fat, skanky cokehead that lives in the building they are working at. I'm calling all the wives so I can put an end to this."

"What? I can't believe it!"

"Well, you better believe it. Your husband is a coke freak." I had seen Hector do coke once with his cousins and thought it was a thing they did occasionally during a party or celebration.

I felt a pain in my chest, and my whole world came crashing down. I was shocked and enraged. I began telling his mother in broken Spanish mixed with English what I had just been told.

Why would he be with someone like that? Why would he be with a fat skank when he has me? I wondered.

I went downstairs to our apartment and started throwing all his clothes into garbage bags. I was blasting music and shaking in anticipation of him coming home. My neighbor Janie from upstairs stopped by. I ranted and raved to her about the entire ordeal. When he came home, I didn't even ask him if it was true.

"Some woman called me on your mom's phone today. She said that you are doing coke and screwing someone that lives in the building that you are working in. I want you to leave. Take your stuff and go back to the slut you are screwing."

He was so surprised that he didn't know what to say. He looked confused, took his stuff, and left.

The next day, Hector was knocking on the door, asking to see the baby. I let him in, and he began to explain.

"That lady that called you is crazy. She doesn't know me. She's just mad at her husband for cheating on her. She called all the wives so that her husband wouldn't be able to say he was hanging out with the guys anymore."

He spoke calmly and seemed to be sincere. I wasn't sure if he was telling the truth, but eventually, I decided to believe him. Things were calm after that, so I figured it was just an isolated incident. I was not prepared for the series of storms that were coming.

Hector got paid on Fridays. On one Friday morning, I reminded him that we needed diapers and some other essentials. He kissed me goodbye and promised that he would come straight home. When he came home, he gave me sixty dollars, then said he was going to the store. I bathed the baby and put him to bed. By ten o'clock, Hector hadn't returned yet, so I went to bed thinking that he probably ran into a friend and was having a beer or two with him. I woke up every hour on the hour and looked at the clock. I had a terrible sinking feeling in my chest. I wondered where he was and who he was with. I became more enraged with every passing hour.

Hector strolled in late morning the next day. I was livid. The anger was building inside me to the point that I thought I was going to explode.

"Where have you been? You need to leave. Go back to wherever you were last night."

"You want me to leave? Okay I'll leave, if you give me back the money that I gave you."

When he was in another room, I tucked the money in my pants. He had spent all his money drinking and getting high all night and had the audacity to ask for the measly sixty dollars back.

"I don't have it," I lied. He stormed into the room and started looking for the money. He emptied drawers, ransacked the closet, and even flipped over the mattress, frantically searching for it.

"Give me the money or else." He threw me on the bed and punched me on my thigh. I had to say something to get him to stop.

"I don't have it. I gave it to my sister to hold for me." A few moments after saying that, the doorbell rang. Hector went to answer the door. It was Megan.

"Hey Megan, where's the money?" he asked. I expected her to ask, "What money?" I was amazed when she answered, "It's upstairs in my mother's apartment." Hector left, and I looked at my thigh. I had a bruise the size of his fist. It wasn't the last time Hector got violent. Our relationship warped into periods of combat and harmony.

Hector was always willing to admit when he was wrong and apologize. He managed to convince me that it wouldn't happen again. We were getting along, and things seemed to be fine for a while. On another Friday morning, Hector woke up and got ready for work as I was making a bottle for the baby. I walked him to the door, and he kissed me goodbye.

"We need milk and diapers. Please buy some on your way home tonight," I asked.

"Okay, I will," he promised.

By dinner time, there was no sign of Hector. It was still early, so I tried not to worry. When I put the baby to bed, I used the last bit of milk and the last diaper. I finally went to bed, hoping that I'd be awakened by the sound of him coming in the door. Once again, I woke up every hour looking at the clock—eleven o'clock, twelve o'clock, one o'clock . . . This time I didn't even care what he was doing or who he was with. I was worried about not having milk for the baby when he woke up in the morning. I hoped that he would waltz in at the last minute. Morning arrived, flooding the room with sunlight. I heard Christopher start to stir. I jumped up and went into the kitchen. I opened the cupboards, frantically searching. I was hoping to find a jar of baby juice that I had missed but there was nothing there. My heart was pounding as the baby started to cry. I found a can of fruit cocktail. I opened it up and poured the thick syrup into his bottle. I added some water to thin it out and fill the bottle. His diaper was soaked, and I didn't have another one. I put a pair of terrycloth training pants coated with plastic on him. I don't remember what I did after that. I probably went up to his mom's apartment to fill the bottle with milk, and I must have borrowed money from someone to buy diapers.

Hector came home nasty and hungover more often, and we fought about it all the time. My dream of a simple, happy life was evaporating. I knew I was in a dangerous situation and felt it was going to end badly.

I watched *The Burning Bed*, starring Farrah Fawcett. It was about a woman who burned her husband in their bed after years of physical and emotional abuse. I identified with the character and found myself fantasizing about killing Hector when he was abusive. I watched him sleep after coming home from a weekend of getting high. I watched him with hatred in my heart. I loathed him. I despised who he had become. I hated my life with him. I hated that he didn't put our son before his own selfishness. I knew I deserved more, but most of all, my son deserved more. I felt like a failure. I had failed as a parent. I brought this beautiful child into the world, and he would suffer. He wouldn't have a good role model, and he wouldn't even have the basic necessities. I had to get out, but I didn't know how. I felt deserted on an island of despair. My marriage became a cycle of tempests, each setting out to erode my self-worth.

Hector's drug use continued to spiral out of control. He gave me less money each month and we fell behind in the rent. We fought each time he came home without a penny in his pocket.

"I hate you. I want a divorce," I yelled.

"I'll kill you if you ever leave me," he warned.

"Well, you might have to kill me, because I'd rather be dead than married to you." He threw me on the bed and ripped off my clothes. He tried to force himself on me.

"Get off me. I hate it. I hate it."

"Shut up," he yelled.

He repeatedly hit me on one side of my face. Then suddenly, he stopped. When I looked at him, I saw horror in his eyes. He jumped up and started crying.

"I'm sorry, I'm sorry." He left the apartment for a few minutes then returned.

"I have a problem, and I need to get help." He said his brother was going to take him to the hospital to get help.

After he left, I got up and went into the bathroom to take a shower. When I looked in the mirror, I saw why Hector had that look of horror in his eyes. The entire left side of my face was black and blue.

I called my dad and asked him if I could borrow twenty dollars. I didn't want him to see my face, so I combed my long, thick black hair to the left side and let it hang over my face. When Dad arrived, I tried to act normal. My tears were ready to break free from behind a dam of shame. I avoided eye contact with him to keep them from erupting. I hoped he wouldn't ask why my hair was hanging over my face. I prayed he wouldn't brush my hair away from my face when he kissed me goodbye. Dad left without knowing about the monster, the marks on my face, or the mess my life had become. When I closed the door behind him, the shame I had been holding in seeped out of my eyes and ran down my face.

Later that day, Tina came down to visit. I felt that I needed a witness to what he was doing. She gasped when I moved my hair away and showed her my face. I told her she could tell her mother if she wanted. I felt the need for his mother to know the truth about him. I didn't want him to twist the truth or deny his actions. Although I showed Tina, I still didn't want my family to know—not yet. It was my problem, and I had to find a way to fix it by myself.

After a couple of days of detox, Hector was back with promises of change. He cried and begged for my forgiveness. For a while, he was on his best behavior. He helped with the baby, helping around the apartment, and coming home with his pay.

The baby was turning one, and I wanted to have a party for him. I needed a day of celebration with family and friends. I wanted to create some fun times and have good memories to look back on. I decided to get Christopher a rocking horse for his first birthday gift. He loved being rocked, and I knew that he would really enjoy it. Hector complained that it was too much money. I thought about all the money he wasted on getting high and ignored his protests and bought it anyway. On the day of the party, Hector disappeared but eventually showed up looking disheveled. He hadn't shaved or showered and wore a cap to cover his uncombed, unwashed hair. Christopher received many gifts, including clothing and toys. The children at the party played games and had lots of fun. We took pictures and made memories of an important milestone in our son's life. I tried to make it a day of normalcy. It was a much-needed distraction from the unhappy life I was living.

In addition to a regular lock, we had a police lock (a steel bar that goes into the floor and leans up against the door to prevent someone from kicking it in). Hector didn't have the key to the police lock, so I started locking him out when he didn't come home. I couldn't just let him come and go as he pleased, leaving us with no money for food. I didn't want him to think he could be out all night, doing whatever he wanted, without any consequences.

Locking him out came with ramifications. If I didn't answer the doorbell, he would bang on the door. Then he would call me, demanding that I open it.

"A*bre la puerta.*" ("Open the door.") The more I ignored him, the louder he got. "*Abre la puerta, abre la* fucking *puerta*! If you don't open the door, I'm going to kill you!" Next, he started to kick the door. The sound of his feet bashing against the door was scarier than his threats. "Go back to whoever you were with last night," I'd sometimes answer. Other times, I ignored him completely while pacing up and down the hallway crying or standing on the other side of the door, listening to him and wondering if I should open the door. There were times that I felt like opening it but was afraid that if I did, he would get violent once he got in. I hoped that a neighbor would call the police, but no one ever did. I waited it out, and eventually, he would retreat. When I heard the elevator coming down, I knew he was going up to his mother's apartment. It was difficult to keep him out all the time. Sometimes, he would catch me going in or out. Other times, he would knock at the door when he got back from work. He was usually well-behaved during the week when he had no money. It was the weekends, when he got paid, that caused the problems.

Tina stayed with us for a brief period while she was looking for an apartment. During that time, she witnessed how violent Hector could be. One day, while we were arguing, Hector rushed up to me and grabbed me by my throat. He had me up against the wall, choking me. I couldn't break free of his grip. Tina was yelling, "Hector, let her go!" I felt like I was going to pass out and just as my eyes started rolling back, he let go. I fell to the floor and told him to get out. He grabbed me by my arm and dragged me across the floor. As he dragged me, my shirt started rolling up. I held my arm over my chest to keep my shirt down.

"I'm going to throw you out this time. Let's see how you like it." He continued dragging me out of the apartment, across the hallway floor, then went into the apartment and locked the door. It was a moment of déjà vu. Feeling humiliated, ashamed, and trapped, I crawled behind the staircase and cried. I thought about my options. I thought about running away, but where would I go? Then, I thought about my son and how Hector wouldn't take care of him or love him the way he deserved. I knew I had to go back for him. After what felt like forever, I swallowed my pride and mustered up the courage to ring the bell. I hoped that if he didn't open the door, his sister would. He opened the door and said, "How do you like being locked out?" I didn't answer. I just walked into the bedroom to check the baby, took a shower, and went to sleep.

In the morning, I had a chain of bruises around my neck. Later that day, I was sitting at Mom's dining room table with Christopher on my lap. I can't remember what the conversation was about, but I distinctly remember saying, "I got choked yesterday." My voice cracked, and my eyes filled with tears. She looked stunned. I moved my hair away from my neck and showed her the bruises. She said, "I don't know why you think you deserve to be treated like that." The fact was, that I didn't think I deserved to be treated that way. I hated the way he treated me and the lack of responsibility he had for our son. I knew it was wrong, but I didn't know how to get out.

"You should file for an order of protection. My sister had to get one because her husband often got violent with her. The police will be able to protect you. He could be arrested if he touches you once you have the order." I knew I had to get him out of the apartment, but I also knew he wouldn't go peacefully. It seemed to be just what I needed. I realized then that I couldn't do it alone.

I took Mom's advice and asked Dad to accompany me to family court to obtain the order of protection. The clerk behind the desk handed me a card. It had a phone number and the words "Victim Services" printed in bold letters. I was taken aback because I had not viewed myself as a victim. It sounded pitiful. Was that what I was?

Dad served Hector with the papers. I told Hector he had to leave and warned him that I would call the police if he was violent with me again.

Hector's mom knocked on my door the next day, asking if she could get his clothing. I looked through the peephole and saw her holding trash bags. I let her in and Hector, who had been hiding in the hallway, barged in behind her.

"Hurry up, get your stuff and get out." I was disgusted with him and had very little patience.

"You are acting like you're pregnant," he said as he walked out of the bedroom with a bag of clothing.

I hadn't even thought that I was acting differently. Maybe I *was* feeling extra cranky. If I was, it was because of all the shit I had to put up with. I started to think about when my last period was, but I couldn't remember. Since I had an irregular cycle, it didn't even occur to me that I could be pregnant. With all the craziness going on, I had lost track. I started listening to my body and thought that maybe I could be pregnant. I made a mental note to go see a doctor soon.

A couple of days later Hector was banging on my door on a Saturday morning around six o'clock. I couldn't call the police because our phone was disconnected. I wasn't going to open the door for him. He began his customary conduct of yelling, cursing, threatening, banging, and kicking the door. I couldn't let him bully me. Tina was sleeping in the living room. "Don't open the door," I whispered.

"Open the door! If you don't open the door, I'm going to break the window!" he threatened. I wasn't sure if he was really going to do it or just trying to scare me into opening the door. I heard Hector yelling from the courtyard. All the windows had child safety gates except the one in our bedroom that housed the air conditioner. I took Christopher out of the crib and handed him to Tina. Since there was a long hallway separating the bedroom from the front door, we would have time to get out before he came in.

"We should stay away from the window and wait here near the door. If we hear glass break, we will have enough time to leave and get to the elevator before he climbs through," I told Tina. She held Christopher in her arms as we waited for the sound of shattered glass. We heard the glass break, opened the door, and headed toward the elevator as planned. It was like a scene from a horror movie. We were frantically hitting the elevator button, but the elevator wasn't coming. While we waited, we heard him screaming my name. We figured that he would soon be in the apartment and would realize we left, come out into the hall, and find us there near the elevator. Tina started running up the stairs with Christopher in her arms.

"When you get upstairs, ring my mother's bell," I told her as I pulled myself up the steps, one by one, toward the second floor. My heart was pounding in my chest as I tried to go as quickly as I could. Tina's aunt lived across the hall from Mom. When I got to the top of the stairs, she was going back and forth, ringing and knocking on both doors. Finally, my mother opened the door with a sleepy look on her face.

"What's going on?" she asked.

"Quick, let us in; he's coming!" I warned. She didn't seem to understand the urgency of the situation.

"He isn't going to come in here," she said calmly.

She led us to her living room and went back to bed. After a few minutes, Tina left and went up to her mom's apartment. I waited until Mom woke up. Mom advised me to call the police and report what had happened.

The police arrived and after listening to my ordeal, they went into my apartment to check it. I hadn't locked the door when Tina and I fled. The police returned to Mom's apartment reporting that the apartment was empty. Hector came down the stairs and said that he wanted to get a few things. The police escorted him into our apartment. I was waiting in Mom's apartment until he was done when we heard a commotion in the hall in front of her apartment.

The cops knocked on the door. Mom opened the door, and Hector was standing there with Lydia.

"I want to see my son. I want to see my baby," he cried.

"Can you let him see the baby?" the officer asked.

Christopher was in his stroller. I wheeled him out into the hallway. Hector picked him up and hugged and kissed him. I saw it as an attempt to manipulate me into feeling sorry for him.

"I bet you are happy. This is what you wanted," Hector said, looking at Mom.

"No, I'm not happy. Seeing my daughter suffer doesn't make me happy," she replied.

When the cops and Hector left, my mother brought Christopher back into the apartment. I was alone with Lydia for a few seconds.

"Is it true? Are you pregnant?" she asked. I couldn't believe he told her that before I even knew if it was true. He probably painted a picture of the out-of-control hormonal woman that was the reason for all the drama.

"I don't know. I could be. I need to go to the doctor and find out," I answered.

When I went back into my apartment, I saw that Hector had tried to break the window but only broke the first layer of the double-paned glass.

A few days later, I asked Megan to watch Christopher. I told her that I might be pregnant and needed to go to the doctor. "If you are, are you going to keep it?" she asked.

I hadn't considered that I didn't have to go through with the pregnancy. I wondered why she had asked me that then I thought about the state my life was in and how having another baby was probably the last thing I needed. We were barely surviving as it was.

I got to the clinic early in the morning. It was a clinic that performed abortions as well as provided pregnancy tests and exams. When I got close to the entrance, protesters were handing out anti-abortion pamphlets.

"Don't kill your baby. Please don't kill your baby," a woman pleaded as she handed me a pamphlet with a picture of an aborted fetus on it.

"I'm just getting a check-up," I said. I walked into the clinic and dropped the pamphlet in a trashcan that was near the door.

"I'd like to have a pregnancy test," I told the woman at the reception desk.

"Do you want to have an abortion? She asked.

"I don't know. I just want to know if I'm pregnant."

"Okay, have a seat until you are called," she directed.

I sat in the chair thinking about what I should do if the test was positive. *I don't want to have an abortion,* I thought. It hadn't even popped into my head until Megan asked me. *But how can I take care of another baby when I'm struggling to take care of the one I have?* Christopher was only fourteen months old. Hector couldn't provide for him. *Oh God, what should I do? Maybe I'm too far along. I hope it's too late.*

My name was called, and I was given a cup to pee in. I took the cup to the bathroom, then returned it to the nurse and sat down. A few minutes later, I was called again and told that the doctor would examine me. After the exam, the doctor said, "You are sixteen weeks. If you wanted an abortion, it's too late."

"That's okay, I didn't want to have one anyway." I answered. I was so relieved. Although my life was in turmoil, I was happy about the life growing inside of me. I knew it was going to be difficult to take care of two babies, but I also knew that I would only get weaker as time went on. It was better to do it now and get the difficult years of caring for babies over with while I was still strong enough. I decided to view this pregnancy as an unexpected blessing.

When I got back to the apartment, I told Megan that I was pregnant and that the baby would be born in the fall. There was a knock at the door, it was Tina. Megan let her in, and they joined me in the kitchen.

"We have some news for you," Megan said.

"What news?" Tina asked.

"You can tell her," I told Megan.

"Christopher is going to have a baby brother or sister."

"What? You're pregnant? Is that why you are wearing that loose shirt?" Tina asked while lifting my shirt up.

"No, I just found out today. The doctor said that I'm four months along, so I guess I'll start showing soon.

"Well, congratulations!"

"It wasn't planned, and I know it's not a good time, but I'm going to make the best of it. It will be nice for Christopher to have a brother or sister to grow up with," I explained.

While Hector and I were separated, he was living upstairs with his mom. I didn't know if he was working, getting high. or coming home, nor did I care. I had peace. I relied on welfare and food stamps to get by. To avoid eviction, welfare helped me catch up with the rent.

A couple of months later, I was at the clinic getting my six-month prenatal checkup when I bumped into Tina.

"Hi. What are you doing here?" I asked.

"I'm here visiting Hector. He had a breakdown. He's in the psychiatric ward in the next building. Do you want to come up and visit him?"

"I don't know."

"Come up with me just to say hi. He will be happy to see you and Christopher."

"Okay," I reluctantly agreed.

When the elevator doors opened, we stepped into the lounge area. There were a couple of table and chair sets and a piano in the room. When Hector saw us, his eyes lit up. He rushed over and touched my belly. The last time he saw me, I wasn't showing. He embraced me, but I left my arms down at my sides. His mom and stepdad were sitting at one of the tables. His mom looked at me with disapproving eyes. I wasn't sure if she was angry at me for throwing him out or upset that I wasn't reciprocating his act of affection. Christopher quickly became the center of attention. Hector scooped him up in his arms kissing and hugging him then brought him over to the piano. Christopher began banging at the keys singing "La, la, la, la, la."

It was strange being near Hector. I felt disconnected from him. He seemed so happy to see us, but I didn't feel the same. I was guarded. While his parents were enjoying Christopher's piano concerto, he took my arm and brought me over to a quiet corner of the room.

"I'm so sorry for everything that I've done. I have a problem but I'm getting help. This time, I'm going to stay until I'm better. I miss you and your big nagging mouth," he joked.

"I love you and Christopher, and I want to be around for the new baby. I want to be there to help you. I want to make up for all the wrong I've done."

"I don't know, I have to think about it," I said.

I thought about our marriage and how we took vows. I wondered if I should stand by him and help him. He accepted me and my flaws. Would it be wrong to walk away without helping him or supporting him? When I got home, I opened my jewelry box. I wanted to look at my wedding ring and hold it. I had taken it off because my fingers were a little swollen from the pregnancy. I was shocked to see that not only was my wedding ring gone, so was my high school graduation ring, my dad's wedding ring, and a ring Ricky had given me. I knew this meant that Hector had sold them for drug money.

A few days later, Lydia shared the details of Hector's breakdown. "He walked into my room and tried to climb out of the window. He was trying to jump. I had to use all my strength to pull him back in. I was screaming for someone to help me. I yelled, 'No, Hector, no.' When we got him in, he put his hand in his pocket and pulled out a few vials of crack. He handed them to me and said, 'Take this from me, please get rid of it.' We called an ambulance, and they brought him to the hospital." She had tears in her eyes as she told me about the frightening ordeal.

A few months prior to Hector's breakdown, I was watching the news with him. There was a segment about how crack cocaine was becoming an epidemic and how addictive it was. There were many horror stories about the crimes and acts of violence associated with the addiction. The addiction was quick, due to the instant euphoria and cheap price. Very often, family members were the victims of these crimes. Addicts were snapping and, in some cases, murdering loved ones. The worst story I heard was of a mother who offered her young daughter to a crack dealer for sex as payment. It was horrifying to think that an addiction could be so strong that people would be capable of such horrendous acts against their family, especially innocent children. I turned to Hector and asked, "Did you ever try that?" He quickly answered, "No, I would never try it." After Lydia told me about his breakdown, I realized that he was probably using it back then.

The revelation that Hector had been using crack explained everything: the violence, staying out all night, spending his entire pay in one night. I remembered the phone call from the wife of his coworker. I wondered when he transitioned from cocaine to crack. I thought about all the verbal altercations we had and all the nasty things I said to him. All along, he was a time bomb. He could have snapped at any time and killed me. I went after him verbally when he was coming down after being high all night. All the while, I had no idea how dangerous the situation really was, and I absolutely had no clue as to the seriousness and depth of an addiction. I didn't understand the hold it had on him and how extremely difficult it was to beat it, nor did I understand the great amount of strength and support a person needed to stay clean.

After weeks of rehab, Hector returned to his mother's apartment. He came down to my apartment asking to see Christopher.

Hector seemed to be his old self again. Eventually, I started to allow him to come down to visit Christopher. He seemed happy and content. He smiled and joked like he did before. When I asked him to leave, he left without a problem. With every visit, he tried to assure me that he was clean and didn't want to use again. He talked about all the bad things he had done and blamed the drugs. Hector was relentless in protesting his love for me. He begged for forgiveness, cried, detested all his wrongdoings, and promised to make amends. Part of me didn't believe him, and part of me wanted to believe him. Deep down inside, all I wanted was to be a family. I wanted someone to share the joy of watching Christopher grow. I wanted a father there for him and for our unborn child. I didn't want to be alone when I gave birth, and I didn't want to bring the new baby home alone. I told myself that maybe it would be different this time since he had gotten professional help. Maybe the breakdown that he had and the possibility of losing his wife and children for good was enough to make him realize how dangerous the drugs were. Maybe he had hit rock bottom and was on his way up for good, and maybe all he needed was someone to love him and give him a chance. Hector knew how important a family was to me, and eventually, he wore me down. He got his job back from the window company and said he would help me by paying the rent. I told him that I would buy the food, buy all the baby's needs (diapers, wipes, and clothing) and pay for the utilities. The deal was he would pay the rent, and I would pay for the rest.

Hector came home most of the time, but I could see that his old ways were starting to creep back slowly. I told him that if he didn't change by the time the baby was born, it would be over. I didn't want my children to grow up with the example that he would be providing.

At times, Hector exhibited paranoid behavior. Once, he walked into our bedroom and looked around as if to catch someone there. Christopher was in his crib, and I was lying on the bed with my huge belly. He opened the closet to see if someone was hiding in it. I was so insulted. I said, "Don't forget to look under the bed," and he looked under the bed. He then walked over to the one window that didn't have the safety gate. It was early fall, and he had taken the air conditioner out of the window. I watched him as he checked the lock.

"You know I have a penny on the lock, and if someone opens the window, the penny will fall. You can put the penny back, but you don't know if I had it on heads or tails." I simply looked at him and replied with, "Did I get it right?" His paranoia led me to believe that he was up to no good and was projecting it onto me.

Living with him was a constant dance of aggression and submission. I felt so alone and lonely. I was trapped in this cycle of good and evil. I tried to do the normal things and get through the days. One night, we were arguing, probably about him staying out or coming home late. He became so angry; he had the look of the devil in his eyes. He bent down close to me and made a fist and put it next to my belly.

"I bet it isn't even mine." I looked at him with astonishment. "Go ahead and say it; say it isn't mine. Say it." All the while his fist was inches away from my belly. I saw evil in his crazed eyes. I knew not to answer sarcastically. I believed that if I did, he would have punched me in my belly. I looked at him with horror. I couldn't believe what he was saying. I wondered who the creature before me was and where the person I once loved had gone. My lip rolled under, and my chin began to quiver. I was blinded by an uncontainable downpour of tears. I sat there trembling and silenced by fear. He stared at me with his wild eyes, then retreated and left the apartment. I don't know why he left. Maybe for a moment, he got a glimpse of the monster he had become in my eyes. Once I heard the door shut, I fell apart on the bed, crying uncontrollably.

Once I had the order of protection, Hector didn't bang on the door. If I didn't let him in, he would call for the elevator to take him up to his mom's apartment. I realized that our marriage would be over soon. I was just biding my time until the baby was born.

Why did I stay with him?

There were normal days sprinkled in with the damaged ones.

There were sunny days spent at the park, swinging the baby on the swings.

There were rainy days when he played with our son at home.

There were days when we shopped together, picking out our favorite foods and anticipating eating them at our table in our tiny kitchen with Christopher next to us in his highchair.

There were mornings that we woke up cuddled in bed with Christopher between us.

There were nights that we laughed while watching TV on the couch together after the baby had fallen asleep.

There were times when we marveled at our beautiful son.

There were times that we thought he was the cutest child on earth as he waddled down the street in tiny outfits.

There were instants that filled our hearts just hearing him call us daddy and mama.

There were times of amusement watching him drag his grandfather's old guitar around, pulling on the strings and singing, "La, la, la."

There were celebrations with family, music, good food, and laughter.

There were days that we listened to music from a boom box while we cleaned our apartment.

There were times when he said I was beautiful.

There were times when I thought he was incredibly handsome.

There were times when I felt safe in his arms as he carried me up the stairs.

There were times when he said he loved me, and I believed him.

When the storm ends, you put it behind you and enjoy the rainbows and sunshine. You try not to think about the next storm. The good days give you hope. They cloud your thinking. They mask the bad and confuse you. They make you believe in things that aren't true. They make you think that love conquers all, that people can change, and that everything will be alright. The bad days make the good days seem even better. They are the dark that welcomes the light. The darker the night . . . the brighter the day.

At seven o'clock in the morning on October 6, I woke up with light contractions. I took a shower, then woke Hector. "Hey, the baby is coming." We got Christopher ready and went up to his mother's apartment to use her phone. I needed to inform my sister, Mary, that the baby was coming, and I would be bringing Christopher to her until I returned from the hospital. Hector's family was trying to guess whether the baby was going to be a boy or a girl. Hector said he wanted a girl, and I thought it would be nice. Hector's brother looked at him and said, "You are wearing a blue shirt, so I think it is going to be a boy." I had the names picked out: Carissa for a girl and Andrew for a boy. I waited a few hours for the contractions to get stronger and closer. Finally, I decided to drop Christopher off and head to the hospital. Hector seemed excited and was being very nice.

After an exam at the hospital, I was told that this baby wasn't as big as the first one and that I most likely would be able to have a natural birth. Hector was in the room with me and was being supportive. My contractions started getting lighter and further apart. The nurses advised me to walk around to bring them back. After walking the halls a bit, the contractions got strong again. I remember the doctor coming in to break my water. The next time the doctor came in, I heard him saying, "She's crowning, she's crowning. Bring her into the delivery room." Soon after I delivered the baby, I heard the doctor exclaim, "It's a boy." As they were cleaning him up, I asked, "How does he look?" Hector was cutting the cord and said, "He's beautiful." The Hector that I fell in love with appeared. He was smiling and happy and sweet. I heard pride in his voice. I thought that maybe our family would survive after all.

They wrapped the baby up and brought him over to me for a quick meeting, then whisked him away to be weighed. "Seven pounds and four ounces," a nurse reported. I was happy that Christopher had a little brother to play with and to grow up with. I got to hold and feed my new baby right away. Once again, I was blessed with a beautiful, healthy son. I was relieved that the pregnancy was over and couldn't wait to go home and introduce Andrew to his brother. Hector visited me every day and seemed to be happy.

The night before I was to go home, I asked Hector to get the room and crib ready for the new baby. I wanted him to wipe down the crib and put the new bedding on it so that it would be ready when we arrived home. I was anxious to see Christopher and have him meet his little brother. Check-out was by eleven o'clock. I hadn't heard from Hector all morning and was getting worried. My bed was needed for another patient. I called Lydia and asked her to go down and knock on the door of my apartment to see if Hector was still there. She said he didn't answer. I was starting to panic because I needed clothes to come home in, and I also needed the baby's clothes to take him home in. Finally, Lydia told me that he answered the door and said he was on his way.

When he walked into the room, I asked, "Why weren't you here earlier? They were about to kick me out of the room." He looked horrible. He reeked of cigarettes and alcohol. He hadn't shaved or showered. He threw the bag of my clothes at me.

"These aren't the clothes that I asked for," I said as I examined them.

"If you don't shut up, I'm going to slap the shit out of you," he warned.

I was so embarrassed and hoped that the other mothers in the room didn't hear him. My eyes welled up. He had that nasty, evil look and tone that I knew too well. I didn't say anything in fear that he would hit me right there in front of everyone. As soon as I got dressed, a nurse wheeled another mother into the room to take my place.

"Let's get out of here. I don't care about this; I just want to see Christopher," he said. It hurt me so much to see him in this state—calling our beautiful new baby "this" and saying he didn't care about him.

"The doctor said that the baby was slightly jaundiced, and they had to put him under a light. We have to wait for the doctor to check him one more time before we can take him home," I informed Hector. We walked over to the nursery to wait for the doctor.

The doctor approached us, and Hector asked him what was going on. He explained what had happened, that the baby was fine, and he approved his discharge. While the doctor was talking, I assumed that he could also smell the stench of alcohol. I was embarrassed by the way Hector looked, smelled, and spoke. I was standing next to him, holding back my tears. My voice shook when I spoke. I felt exposed and naked as if he could see the sadness and disgrace that I was feeling. I was imagining what he must have been thinking. Would he go home that night and tell his wife or family about us and feel sorry for the baby? I was yelling inside my head, saying, *This isn't me; I'm not like him.* Maybe he didn't notice how he looked or didn't smell the alcohol. If he did, he could have thought he looked and smelled that way because he was out celebrating the birth of his son. I felt like a loser by association. I probably was projecting my feelings onto the doctor.

On the cab ride home all I could think about was how disgusted I was and how I wanted Hector out of my life for good. I just wanted to bring my baby home, have my sister bring Christopher over, and then I could get rid of him. I got through the pregnancy and knew that it was over. I swore to myself that the first time he walked out of the apartment, I would lock him out for good. I would take care of my babies alone. I was ready for it. I knew that I could do it.

When we pulled up in front of the building, I saw Megan at the entrance of the building. She ran over to the car and exclaimed, "There's a marshal at your door, locking up your apartment." I was confused and stunned. We walked into the building and saw the marshal getting ready to padlock our door.

"Get whatever you need. I'm going to take an inventory of the rest and then I'll be locking up the apartment because you are being evicted," he informed us.

While I was in the hospital, Hector received a three-day dispossess notice. If he had gone down to the housing court, he would have been given a court date, and we could have tried to come up with the money or be given a date to move out. Instead, Hector did nothing. He got high for the three days that I was in the hospital. He ignored the notice, and if you don't answer in court, an eviction will follow.

I walked into the apartment and down the hall to my bedroom and sat on my bed. As I sat there holding my newborn, the gravity of the situation started to sink in. I caught a glimpse of myself from the mirror on the closet door. I saw a girl with puffy eyes and black streams of mascara running down her cheeks. She was a stranger, an unknown character in this tragedy. She was not me. She couldn't be. How did she get here? What happened to the intelligent person who had dreams of becoming a teacher and a mother? Who replaced her with this pitiful victim looking back at me in the mirror? I looked down at my three-day old son and thought, *What a terrible homecoming for my sweet baby. What a failure I am.* I felt so humiliated, so degraded, and so betrayed. At twenty-three, it was the lowest point in my life. The marshal once again instructed us to grab as much as possible before he padlocked the apartment. I looked at the crib and saw that it was dusty and empty. It was another broken promise. Hector hadn't cleaned or prepared the crib for the arrival of the new baby. I could imagine what he'd been doing during those three days.

I turned to Hector and sarcastically said, "We won't get thrown out of here; they can't throw us out."

The marshal heard me saying that and said, "Oh yes, you can get thrown out, and you better believe it, because it is happening now." He probably thought I was in denial.

I turned to him and said, "I'm just repeating what was told to me." Hector looked at me for a moment, then turned to the dresser to retrieve some clothing.

I sat immobilized in the eye of the storm as a whirl wind of chaos began. Everyone started seizing things. We didn't have time to get boxes or even bags to carry items of importance.

Hector threw sheets and blankets on the floor and dumped the contents of drawers from the dresser onto them, then tied them in knots. Megan, Lydia, and Luis were there with us. Luis and my sister were trying to take the crib apart. Hands were everywhere snatching my belongings.

"Stop touching my stuff; leave it alone!" I yelled.

"We need to get the important stuff out. We need the babies' things," they explained.

"Where will we put everything?" I asked.

"You can come upstairs with us," Lydia said.

"You can stay with me," Megan answered. She had an apartment on the fourth floor across from Nanny that she shared with a roommate. It was a one-bedroom apartment. Her roommate converted the living room into a bedroom, and they shared the bathroom and the kitchen.

Although Lydia offered, I knew that I couldn't go to Hector's family's apartment. I couldn't live with him, not after the way he treated me in the hospital and not after this. I had said that I would leave him if he didn't change by the time the baby was born, and I also said that if we lost the apartment, the relationship would be over. It was the point of no return for me. There would be no hope of repairing our relationship and no dreams of better tomorrows for our family. There was no amount of light to remedy the darkness of that day.

When the violence of the storm wipes away all you have built,
When the warmth of lies no longer soothes you,
When dreariness outweighs joy,
When you realize your dreams are yours alone,
It is time to leave.

My clothing and the children's belongings were brought up to Megan's apartment. My living room set, bed, and kitchen table were left and locked up in the apartment by the marshal.

Megan's bedroom had a twin bed in the middle of the room. We placed the crib on one side of the bed for Andrew and the playpen on the other side for Christopher. Megan offered me her bed and slept on the floor. I hoped that it would be temporary and that I could get my apartment back. After I got settled, I called Mary and asked her to bring Christopher to Megan's apartment. I said that I would explain when she got there. It was the first time since Christopher was born that we were separated. I missed him and couldn't wait to hold him and introduce him to his little brother. When Mary rang the doorbell, I rushed to the door and took him from her arms. He wrapped his legs around me, and I kissed his cheeks while I walked down the long hallway toward the bedroom. She said, "Be careful, don't carry him. You just had a baby." Ignoring her, I brought him over to the crib and showed him his baby brother. I needed some normalcy. I had dreamed of the moment that he would meet his little brother. I couldn't let the turmoil that was going on take that moment away. It would be hard enough for him to undergo new living arrangements, the addition of a new baby, and the absence of his father (although it was for the best). Christopher was nineteen months old. I leaned him over the crib to see his brother. "See the baby? His name is Andrew. Say Andrew. Can you say Andrew?" I asked. He uttered, "Ado." My sisters looked on with sadness as the joyful moment occurred in the midst of anguish and chaos. Bringing the children together made my life feel less fragmented.

Chapter 5

 Moving On

I woke up in a room chilled with October air, my newborn fast asleep on my chest. Megan was asleep on the floor at the bottom of the bed; Christopher was stirring in his playpen to the right of me. As my eyes focused, a sinking feeling came over me as the daunting reality of my situation persisted.

Resting and bonding with my baby was a luxury I had to relinquish. Mary was on her way over to help Megan watch the children while I desperately tried to fix the situation that Hector put us in. I took a cab downtown to Livingston Street to the Housing Court, in an attempt to get my apartment back. "The only way to fight the eviction is to come up with the full amount owed," a clerk informed me. As I stood on the corner waiting for a cab back to Megan's apartment, I watched the people on the street walking by. They all seemed to be carefree. I was tired from waking up every two hours during the night to feed the baby. My breasts ached because my milk had just come in. I was emotionally exhausted.

A guy passing by stopped, turned around, and smiled at me. I rolled my eyes at him and turned away. *What is he looking at?* I thought. *Why is he smiling?* It made me realize that I appeared to be just another citizen going about my day like everyone else on the street. I didn't appear to have just given birth four days earlier. I didn't look like a homeless person, nor did I appear to be the wife of an abusive drug addict. No one could tell I was afraid that SMA would affect my ability to take care of my kids. No one would have guessed that I was using all my strength to keep it together, trying not to cry on that corner, trying not to think about the shame that I felt. That smile from a stranger reminded me that all that had happened hadn't really change who I was. It wouldn't define me. This was just a phase, an occurrence, a moment that would pass. It wasn't a scarlet letter that would follow me. It would be behind me soon. I thought about my children. I had to hold them. They needed me. I must be strong for them. I must survive this for them. It was all about them.

When I got back, I went to Nanny's apartment and called my caseworker at the welfare center. "We can only give you a portion of the rent owed. You will need to come up with the balance," I was told. They couldn't give me all the money because they had helped me when Hector was in rehab a few months prior.

When I walked into Megan's apartment, Dad was there to drive Mary home. Christopher ran over to me. I peeked into the crib and saw Andrew fast asleep. I sat on the bed so Christopher could climb on my lap.

"What happened at court?" they asked.

"They said that I have to pay all that is owed to stop the eviction, but my case worker can only give me part of it."

"Why did you have another baby?" asked Dad.

"What does that matter now?" I answered.

When Dad and Mary left, Mom came up and asked if I got in touch with the Welfare department. I explained to her what they said.

"Give me the number. I want to talk to her," she demanded.

"She will tell you the same thing that she told me," I said. "Give me the number," she insisted. I gave her the number and felt like a child whose mother wanted to call the school and speak to the teacher directly because she didn't believe that her daughter really didn't have homework. I thought that maybe if she heard it directly from the case worker, she would understand how desperate my situation was and offer to help. After she spoke to the woman, she relayed the information that I had already heard and added, "You will have to go to a welfare hotel."

"I would never go to a welfare hotel. I have other choices." I had heard stories that welfare hotels were dangerous rundown buildings that were inundated with drugs and crime. "I'd rather stay with friends or even go up to Hector's mom's apartment before I live in a welfare hotel."

"They don't want you up there," Mom replied.

"Yes, they do; they offered to take me in. I just don't want to be near Hector," I answered.

Hector was in his mother's place with no concerns or responsibilities. As I frantically worried about where I would live with my babies, no one offered to give me the money for the rent, and I dared not ask. They probably thought that I would take him back and find myself in the same situation. I didn't blame them. There was no reason for them to believe me this time. My only option was to stay with my sister until I could find another apartment.

Shortly after the eviction, Hector came to me and said that he had asked someone in the building to store my furniture in an empty room of his. This would prevent the landlord from putting our stuff in a warehouse somewhere. "Why would he do that for you? Did you give him some money?" I asked. "Yes, I gave him a few bucks," he answered. I was relieved that I wasn't going to lose all my belongings. By the end of the month, Megan's roommate moved out. I moved into her room and started to pay her share of the rent.

I asked Hector to get my furniture and move it into my room. My couch, loveseat, and end tables were placed on one side of the room; the kitchen table with its detached legs were propped up against the wall, and the chairs were stacked in a corner. On the other side of the room was my bed, dresser, and the baby's crib. I was grateful to have all my belongings with me.

I was lonely and sad living in that room, but at the same time, I was at peace. All I had to worry about was taking care of the babies. I no longer lived in fear of Hector and his outbursts. One day, while the kids were taking a nap, I went to throw the garbage out down the hall. On my way back, I heard footsteps coming down the stairs. I looked over and saw Hector. We hadn't seen each other in weeks. He rushed over to me and said, "I miss you and Christopher so much. How's the baby? Can I see him?" I was afraid that someone in my family would see him near me. I didn't want them to think that I was going to take him back. Although he had done so many horrible things, I thought that he should see his sons. Megan had been staying at her boyfriend's house a lot, so I let Hector in. He smiled at Andrew and said, "Oh, he's beautiful! He looks like you." He picked him up and kissed him. Christopher woke up and was very excited to see him. Hector was like Dr. Jekyll and Mr. Hyde. When he was good, he was really good. He smiled and laughed and had a charming personality. It felt good to watch him interact with our children. For a few moments we were a family, and it felt good, but I knew it was a farce. He was incapable of being the husband that I wanted or the father they needed. He looked around the room and noticed that I didn't have a television. He said, "I'll be right back." and returned a few minutes later with a black-and-white, thirteen-inch television, placed it on the dresser, and plugged it in.

"Do you need help with anything?" he asked.

I had been anxious about the baby's upcoming appointment. "Well, the baby's appointment is coming up, and it will be very hard for me to go alone. I won't be able to manage with both of them, especially with folding and unfolding the stroller."

"I'll ask my mom to watch Christopher, and I'll go with you to the appointment." I was happy that he was going to help me. If he couldn't help me financially, at least he could help with the kids occasionally.

On the day of the appointment, I brought Christopher upstairs so his grandmother could watch him, and we headed to the clinic. He helped me with lifting, opening, and closing the stroller. At the check-up, he lifted the baby out of the stroller and onto the examination table. Together, we watched as the doctor weighed and examined our newborn. When we arrived back at the apartment building, he opened the stroller, helped me put the baby in, and carried it up the steps to the elevator, all things that would be impossible for me to do alone.

"Why don't you spend the day with me? I want to spend time with the kids, and I want to talk about us making it work," he asked as we waited for the elevator to come down. I was being strong and doing fine without all the drama, and I knew that he hadn't changed. There was no way I was going to go back with him.

SMA would continue to hinder my ability to do certain things independently. I wished that I could rely on him occasionally for what little support he could give without being a couple. It became apparent that he probably only went with me with the hopes that he could break me down and manipulate me into falling for his lies. We had participated in that dance many times before. He pleaded while we waited for the elevator to come. When he saw that I was adamant about not wanting to spend time with him, he got angry. When the elevator came, he shoved the stroller into the elevator in such a violent way that it crashed into the back wall. The baby got startled and shook.

"What's wrong with you? Be careful. You scared him. He's just a newborn." We argued on the ride up to his mother's apartment. He said something nasty to me. Once again, Dr. Jekyll was repressed, allowing Mr. Hyde to emerge. The ugly, alternate personality disgusted me. Upon leaving the elevator, I snapped, "You're such a lowlife!" My comment enraged him, causing the true monster to become unchained. Without warning, he rushed up to me and pushed me so hard that I went flying across the stone floor, landing on my hip. I yelled out in pain, then he rushed over and picked me up with a concerned look on his face. He was probably worried that I would call the police on him. I went into his mother's place, got Christopher, and went back to my sister's apartment. As the day went on, the pain in my hip increased.

It got so bad that it became painful for me to walk. I was afraid that something was broken and I needed to go to the hospital.

I asked my sister if she would watch the babies while I went to the hospital. She said no, so I went upstairs and told Lydia what had happened.

"Can you watch them for me while I get my hip checked?" I asked.

"Okay, I'll be down in a few minutes," she promised. A few minutes later, Lydia knocked on the door.

"Hi." I said, opening the door with a smile. Lydia had a serious look on her face.

"I'm sorry, but I'm not going to be able to watch the kids for you," she said.

"Why?" I asked.

"My mother said that I shouldn't help you because you could get Hector in trouble if you go to the hospital and make a report. So, if I help you, it's like I'm helping you to get him in trouble."

My eyes welled up. I couldn't believe that they were protecting him.

"I wasn't going to make a report against him. I just want to make sure my hip is okay."

"I'm sorry, but my mother said not to babysit for you."

"Okay," I said, then shut the door.

"Megan, please watch the kids while I go to the hospital. My hip is hurting badly. I asked Lydia to watch them, but she said her mother won't let her." Megan finally agreed.

At the emergency room, an X-ray was taken. The doctor reported that my hip was bruised but nothing was broken. I limped around for a few days until the pain eventually went away.

I had to accept that I was alone in caring for my children and that Hector was incapable of providing any support whatsoever.

Christmas was very lonely. I dressed Andrew in a little red outfit and sat him in his infant seat. I bought a couple of toys for Chris to open. On New Year's Eve, I watched Dick Clark's countdown. After the ball dropped, I kissed Christopher, who was asleep beside me, and whispered "Happy New Year" in his ear. Then, I leaned over the crib and kissed Andrew, whispering in his ear as well. I heard the noise of neighbors bringing in the New Year. Hearing their cheers and horn blowing made me feel isolated. I knew that only two floors above, my in-laws were celebrating with delicious traditional Puerto Rican food and listening to festive music. I knew that if I went up there, I would be welcomed, but I also knew that I had to stay away from Hector.

I looked out the window on a cold day in mid-January. The sky was gray, and snow was beginning to fall lightly. I was running low on milk and formula and wanted to get to the store and back before the weather got worse. I asked Megan if she could watch the kids while I went to the store. She said she was waiting for her boyfriend and didn't want to. I asked her if she could go for me when he came, but she said they had to go somewhere and didn't have time to stop at the store.

The snow was starting to stick, and I knew that it was only going to get worse, so I decided to take the babies with me and head out. I put a plastic cover on the stroller and dressed Christopher in his snowsuit. I helped Christopher walk down the four steps leading to the entrance of the building, then I pulled the stroller down backwards and headed out. By the time I got out of the supermarket, there was about three inches of snow on the ground. The snow was coming down heavily and accumulating quickly. The wheels of the stroller stopped turning. I had to use my weight to push the stroller through the snow. Christopher held onto the side of the stroller and the milk and formula were on top. I turned the corner, and saw Megan exit the building and get into her boyfriend's car. When I reached the building, a neighbor happened to be coming in. He grabbed the stroller and carried it up the stairs that led to the elevator. As we waited for the elevator, my hair turned from white to black as the snow melted on my head. I walked into the apartment with a sense of accomplishment. I had to get used to doing things for myself, no matter how difficult it was.

Megan spent most of her time at her boyfriend's house. I was alone in the apartment, existing solely as a mother by making bottles, changing diapers, and washing clothes. The days began to blur and blend into each other. I rarely went out and had very little contact with others.

The actors on television became my friends. They were always there, ready for me when I tuned in. I watched family shows and escaped into a world of normalcy portrayed by actors. The fathers were always present. They had jobs and took part in raising their children.

In late January, Megan came back to the apartment and informed me that she was pregnant and going to get married soon. "You are going to have to find an apartment. I'm going to be living here with my husband, and you can't be living here with us."

It was very difficult to look for an apartment. I needed someone to watch the two babies so that I could go out looking. Even if I found a babysitter, no one wanted to rent to a young single mother of two without a job. Once, I went to a real estate agency with my brother-in-law, pretending to be a couple, but was unsuccessful in finding an apartment.

On February 28, the day before Christopher's second birthday, Megan came back to the apartment and said, "I want you to leave. I told you that I wanted my apartment back. You have to leave," she demanded.

"I haven't been able to find an apartment. Besides, I've been paying rent here and couldn't save," I explained.

"I don't care. I want you out, and if you don't leave, I'll call the police and have them throw you out."

I told Mom what was happening, and she said that she wasn't going to get involved. So, I called Dad.

"Hi Daddy, Megan wants me to leave. Can you come over and drive me to my friend's house?"

"What? She's not going to throw you out."

"Well, she said that she's going to call the police and have me thrown out."

"I'll be right over."

He rushed over with the intent of talking sense into her.

"What's going on?" he asked after I let him in.

"I want her to leave. I want my apartment back," Megan answered.

"How could you throw your sister out on the street with two babies? If you go through with this, you are no daughter of mine."

"I don't care," she answered.

"You bitch, don't ever talk to me again."

"That's fine with me," answered Megan.

"I'm sorry that I can't take you in. It's not my place." Dad was living in a condo with Judy, my little sister, and his mother-in-law, and there wasn't room for three more people. Mom didn't invite us to stay with her, and I didn't ask.

About a month or two after Andrew was born, my former neighbor Janie came back to the building to visit Lydia. When she asked for me, Lydia told her where I was living. Janie knocked on Megan's apartment door. I was surprised to see her. I was pregnant with Andrew the last time we saw each other. I let her in and showed her the baby. She looked around the room at all the furniture and bags piled in corners.

"If you ever need a place to stay, let me know. I have a six-room apartment." I remember thinking that I would never be in a situation where I would have to stay with her. But now, with nowhere to go, Janie's invitation popped into my head, but I didn't know her address and she didn't have a phone. I called Lydia from Nanny's apartment to see if she had Janie's address.

"She lives over a deli, but I don't have the address with me. It's at work in my address book. I can give it to you on Monday," she said.

It was Saturday and I needed a place to stay until I could get Janie's address. I called my friend Yolanda and asked if I could stay with her for a couple of days. Yolanda agreed, and Dad drove us to her apartment.

She lived in a studio apartment with her boyfriend and four-year-old son. When I arrived at Yolanda's apartment, she removed her son from his bed and laid him on hers so that Christopher and I could sleep on his twin bed. Andrew slept in his stroller next to us.

The next day Yolanda baked Christopher a cake, and we sang "Happy Birthday" to him. I was glad that he was too young to know that his birthday was being celebrated under such sad conditions. It had been five months since the eviction, and we were homeless again.

On Monday, I called Lydia and got Janie's address. Dad came over when he got off work to drive us to her place. I thanked Yolanda for her kindness and generosity. Dad gathered our things and loaded them in his car.

Since Janie didn't have a telephone, I was unable to ask before heading over. As we neared her residence, the deli sign flashing on the building was a beacon in the dark night. Dad parked under the elevated train. I asked him to wait in the car with the kids while I found out if we would be able to stay with her. A train rattled by above me as I exited the car. All I had was the hope that a stranger would honor something she had said in passing. I didn't have a plan B and hoped she remembered her offer and was still able to follow through with it. The door to the building was unlocked, so I let myself in and climbed up the stairs to her second-floor apartment. I knocked on her door and was greeted by a white-haired man in his sixties. When I asked for Janie, he informed me that she was working downstairs in the deli. I went back downstairs and entered the deli. I didn't see her, so I walked down the length of the long counter to the end, where I found her laughing and talking with her coworkers behind the counter. When our eyes met, I forced a smile. She walked over to me and looked into my glassy eyes. I stood before her like a book that had been thrown open, with words of sorrow and desperation written across the pages.

"Where are the kids?" She asked before I could muster up the courage to speak.

"In the car with my dad," I replied.

"Let's go, I'll take you upstairs."

When we left the deli, I waved for Dad to bring the kids. He carried Andrew up the stairs for me then went back down to get the bags. When he returned, he thanked her for taking me in. I thanked him and kissed him goodbye. Janie introduced me to Victor. He was a family friend who watched her kids at night while she worked. Janie told me to make myself comfortable while she ran back downstairs to finish her shift.

I sat on her futon and gave the kids a bottle of milk. They both fell asleep quickly. Her sink was overflowing with dishes. It looked like every cup, plate, and utensil that she owned was dirty. There wasn't any room for me to wash out the babies' bottles, so I washed all her dishes. When she came home, she was surprised to see the kitchen clean. "You didn't have to do the dishes." I responded with, "It's nothing; it's the least I could do."

I filled her in about my sister putting us out and that I couldn't go back to Hector. She understood because she was separated from her husband, who also was abusive. Janie's husband would beat her so badly that she would be left bedridden for days. She was forced to rely on family and friends to help take care of her kids. Janie had two sons. The oldest, Nicholas—Nicky, as she called him—was seven. Christian, Janie's youngest, was about fifteen months old.

So, there we were, two mothers of two boys who were separated from our violent husbands. I offered to pay Janie some rent for letting us stay with her. "No, keep your money and save it for your next apartment. Just chip in for the food," she said. Janie laid clean sheets on the futon, which became a place of refuge for me and my boys.

I didn't know how long it would take to find an apartment, so I decided to have Andrew christened a couple of weeks after moving in with Janie. After the ceremony, Mom stopped by Janie's apartment to drop off a cake. Before she rushed out, she told me to call her for help looking for an apartment.

After I served the cake, I smiled for Dad's camera with my newly baptized baby. When the pictures were developed, I gazed at our first portrait as a trio. I couldn't help feeling that the photo was incomplete, that they were too young to be without a father. Every birthday, holiday, and special event will have a void in the photograph. I thought about the questions that I would have to answer one day. *Who is my father? When did you break up?* "We broke up when Andrew was three days old," I'd have to say one day. *Why did you break up?* Could I tell them the harsh truth, or would I come up with a lie to protect them? I thought I'd probably tell them the truth one day; maybe when they were old enough to handle it.

Mom was in contact with a real estate agent and would relay messages from her to me. I called her from a pay phone on the corner every couple of days. To increase my chances of getting an apartment, she asked her cousin, Tom (the one that helped me get my first job), to say that I worked for him at his employment agency. After four weeks at Janie's, Mom informed me of an apartment that was available. I called the agent and got the information. I asked Janie to watch Andrew and jumped in a cab with Christopher to see the apartment. My only request was to have an apartment on the first floor. I was told that it was a second-floor apartment. I really didn't want to have to deal with stairs, especially since Andrew was still an infant. I knew that carrying him upstairs would be impossible, but I went to see the apartment anyway.

The apartment was in a section of Brooklyn called Bath Beach. As I pulled up in front of the building, I noticed a stoop with five steps leading up to the entrance. I rang the bell of one of the tenants to get in.

"Are you here to see the apartment?" she asked, looking down from the second floor.

"Yes."

"Okay, I'll give you the key when you come up," she said.

The vestibule was dark, and the stairs were steep. Christopher was scared and didn't want to go up. I started climbing the stairs in my usual way, using the railing to pull myself up.

"No, mama, no,"

"It's okay, baby, come on."

The woman was looking down, watching me go up step by step. It probably seemed like I was climbing that way because I was waiting for my toddler to catch up.

The fear of being alone in the dark hallway was stronger than the unknown that was before him, so he reluctantly followed me. When I reached the second floor, the woman handed me a key.

"Hi, I'm Joyce. My dad lives here. I'm just visiting him. The apartment is upstairs on the left."

"Oh, I was told it was on the second floor," I said, disappointed.

"No, I guess they got confused because the first apartments are on the second floor since they are over a business." There was a storefront on the street level, with the entrance around the corner.

"Okay, thanks. I'll return the key on my way out," I answered. By now, Christopher was next to me. We climbed up the next flight together. As soon as I stepped into the apartment, there was a bedroom to the left and a bathroom opposite it on the right; straight ahead was the kitchen and beyond the kitchen was the living room. The kitchen was a good size, but it looked worn and dated and lacked a refrigerator. To the left of the kitchen was an opening leading to a small room. This was the second bedroom, but the previous renters had opened the wall to make a dining area. I knew I could close it up with vinyl doors one day. The bathroom was small, dark, and dirty. It had a tiny catty-cornered sink, and there was a big crack in the floor near the threshold. The kitchen had beat-up linoleum, and all the other rooms had bare wood floors. The floors had chips and cracks and were speckled with paint. They were in such bad shape that sanding them was not an option. It was not as big or as nice as my last apartment, and it needed a lot of work. Although the apartment wasn't in the greatest condition, I imagined that I could fix it up, but the stairs were going to be a big challenge.

When I got back to Janie's place, I described the apartment, and I mentioned my concerns about the stairs. "But you have to take it," she answered. I knew she was right. I didn't want to overstay my welcome at Janie's, and I was desperate. Not many people would be willing to rent to me, so I decided to tell the agent that I was interested in it. I thanked Janie for her kindness and asked her to promise me that she wouldn't tell anyone where I lived, not even my sisters-in-law. I couldn't take the chance that their loyalty to Hector would come before my wishes.

    I saved up one month's rent while I stayed with Janie, and my parents each gave me a month's rent, one for the security deposit and one for the agency fee. I met the landlord and agent at the apartment a few days later. The landlord was a short, stocky Italian immigrant. He owned a few properties in the neighborhood. I explained my concerns about the condition of the bathroom and the furniture left behind by the previous renters. The landlord agreed to make repairs to the bathroom and to remove the furniture. When I asked for the lease, he said, "No lease, I don't want welfare." My eyes widened with surprise. I was speechless because I knew that without a lease, I wouldn't be eligible for public assistance. Before I could say anything, the agent defended me. "Come on Joe, she's not on welfare. She needs the security of a lease because she's a mother." I was equally surprised that she defended me because the first time that I went to see the apartment, she had informed me that she called the agency that my cousin worked at and whomever answered the phone said that I didn't work there. Apparently, Tom was out the day they called, and someone answered his line. I'm not sure if she felt sorry for me or just wanted her commission, but thanks to her, the landlord agreed, and we signed a one-year lease for 425 dollars a month.

    I moved into my apartment at the beginning of April. My cousin and Mom's husband helped move my furniture out of Megan's apartment. The first thing I did when I entered the apartment was check the bathroom. I was disappointed to see that the landlord hadn't made any repairs. When I walked into the living room, the old furniture was still left behind. We had to pile my furniture up on one side of the room because there wasn't enough space with the discarded furniture in the room. After they left, I unpacked the essentials and put sheets on the crib and on my bed. The place was cold and dusty and lacked the feeling of home. I looked around and made a mental note of what needed to be cleaned. I put a small container of milk out on the windowsill until I was able to get a refrigerator.

The night before I moved, I told Janie, "I'm worried about not having a refrigerator. I can ask my dad to take me shopping for a refrigerator, but I won't be able to call him since I don't have a phone, and I won't be able to get up and down the stairs with the baby to use a payphone. There's a salvage place near my mom that sells appliances. They sell overstocked items that are less expensive."

"I'll have Victor check on you tomorrow. He can drive you to your mom's place," she promised. Victor showed up in the morning and carried the baby down the stairs to his car. He drove us to Mom's building, fifteen minutes away. He helped me get the stroller up to the elevator. I asked him to wait in the hall until Mom answered, just in case she wasn't home. Mom opened the door and said, "What do you want now?" On the day of the move she warned, "I hope you don't find yourself in the same situation." I knew she was annoyed with me.

"I need to call Daddy so that I can ask him to help me get a refrigerator." She opened the door and walked down the hall toward her living room. I went into the kitchen and called Dad.

"Hi Daddy, can you take me to get a refrigerator? I'm at Mom's and there's a place that sells them cheap near here."

"Okay, I'll be there in a little while."

Dad lived about ten minutes away by car. After we purchased the fridge, he drove us home. When we got to the apartment, he carried the baby up the stairs for me, then went back down and hauled the refrigerator up the stairs with a hand truck and placed it in the kitchen. I removed my milk from the windowsill and put it in the refrigerator. I asked him to take me food shopping. He carried the baby down the stairs and back up when we got back. He lugged all the shopping bags up all the steps, making two to three trips. Once again, I thanked him for helping me. I was happy to have a refrigerator and food. When he left, I felt surrounded by loneliness. I felt trapped and isolated in a neighborhood miles from family and friends. Without a telephone, I was unable to ask anyone for help. The uncertainty of how I would manage living alone on the third floor stirred feelings of anxiety and fear.

A couple of weeks later, I was out of some essential items and needed to go to the supermarket. I made my way down the stairs by placing Andrew in a carrier that Janie gave me. I put him in it while he was in the crib, then lifted him up and over the crib railing while it was attached to me. Gravity made going down the stairs possible, but I had to go very slowly and carefully. I made my way to the pay phone around the corner.

"Hi, Daddy. Can you come by and help me go to the store? I ran out of milk." I asked.

"I can't go there every time you need help. I'm not your husband," he answered.

I felt so hurt because I knew that I was a burden but had no other option but to call him. It took all my strength to get down the stairs with the baby attached to me. There was no way I could get back up with the baby, never mind a bag of groceries.

"I know you aren't my husband; I have a husband, but I can't call him. If I call him, I'll never get rid of him. Forget it. Sorry that I bothered you." I was about to hang up when he answered, "I'll be there in a few minutes." I walked over to the building and waited on the stoop until he arrived.

After that day, Dad came by once a month to take me to the supermarket to do the big shopping. Every time, it was the same routine. He carried the baby down, then back up the stairs and placed him in his crib while I pulled myself up, with Christopher walking in front of me. Then, he would haul up the groceries. Eventually, he got me a shopping cart so that he only had to make one trip up the steps.

I had enough food stamps to buy food, but I didn't have enough cash for the nonfood items. If I went over my limit, he would pay the difference. Sometimes he looked annoyed. He rolled his eyes and sighed, but he still paid. Dad also stopped by periodically to check on us. He'd walk into the babies' room to see if I was low on diapers. Then he'd open the fridge to see if there was enough milk. If not, he would say, "I'll be right back" and head to the store, returning with the much-needed items.

Early one evening, a couple of weeks after I moved in, my bell rang. When I stepped into the hallway, my neighbors were also looking down to see who had rung their bells. It was Lydia and she was asking, If I lived there. I looked down the stairwell, surprised to see her. I invited her in and asked how she found me.

"I stopped by Janie's to see how you were. When she said that you had moved, I asked her for your address. She told me that you didn't want us to know where you were, and she promised you that she wouldn't tell anyone. I begged her to tell me, and I promised her that I wouldn't tell Hector where you live. She said that she didn't know the exact address but gave me the cross streets. So, I rode my bike here and went into every building on the four corners of the intersection, ringing bells until I found you. My brother is a jerk; I would never tell him where you are."

"I'm sorry, but I wasn't sure if you would side with him," I explained.

"I would never side with him again. I know he's no good, and I want to be part of my nephews' lives, even if he isn't."

The kids were asleep, but I let her peek in on them. I showed her the apartment and shared my ideas for fixing it up.

"Can I tell Tina where you live?" she asked before she left.

"Only if she promises not to tell Hector," I warned.

A few days later Tina came with her four-month-old daughter. Tina was separated from her daughter's father, who was also abusive. They stayed with us for a few days. I got in touch with the landlord and reminded him about getting rid of the unwanted furniture. After he removed it, she helped me arrange my furniture, which was still piled up in the living room. With the furniture in place, I really started to see the potential.

Tina came back and spent Mother's Day with us. My next-door neighbor Diana had told me to let her know if I ever needed anything, so we asked her if she had a radio we could borrow. We turned it on and waited for the DJ to play the song "I'll Always Love My Mama" by the Intruders. We sang together in the kitchen. It was our first Mother's Day as single moms. After serenading the kids, we brought them to the park. We pushed Chris on the swing then watched him run around while we sat on benches in the sun as the babies napped. It was the first time that I was able to get out of the apartment to enjoy the warm weather. It was nice having her visit us during those early days of isolation.

In June, the landlord informed me that my downstairs neighbor, who was a contractor, would be renovating my bathroom. I had to live through the demolition and construction and would be without a working bathroom for a few days. I bathed the kids in the kitchen sink. My neighbor Diana left her key with me so that I could use her toilet and shower while she was at work.

When the bathroom was finally done, it was beautiful. The floor was covered in light blue tiles that matched the tiles in the shower. It felt great bathing my kids in a clean, brand-new tub. The bathroom was extended into a hall closet, which made it large enough for a full-sized sink and vanity. With the only closet gone, Mom and her husband built a closet for me in the small room off the kitchen that I claimed as my own. Dad laid new linoleum in the kitchen. My friend Jr., (who stood as a witness when Hector and I got married) worked for a flooring company and installed new linoleum in my living room and laid my remnant carpet in the kids' room as a favor. With all the dirty, disheveled floors covered, my apartment felt clean and cozy. Lydia and her friend painted my kitchen for me. The once run-down apartment was finally a home.

After paying my rent, I was left with only fifty dollars a month in cash. Dad had offered to pay the electric and gas bills. One day while Dad was visiting, he insisted that I get a telephone. "You need to have a phone. What if there's an emergency? What if something happens to you or one of the kids? You can't be here alone with two babies and no phone." I explained that I couldn't afford a phone. He replied with, "I'll pay for it, just don't run up the bill." I was grateful to have such a generous father. Once I called him because I was out of money. He sounded so happy to hear from me. I realized that I hadn't called him just to see how he was in a while. We made small talk and tears flowed as I listened to his voice, too ashamed to ask for money.

Although I felt blessed that he was helping me, I felt bad that I wasn't independent and continued to feel like a burden. Eventually the local market offered a delivery service. I was pleased to be able to go shopping without bothering him. It was one less thing that I had to depend on him for.

Without Dad to bail me out when I was short at the register, I had to make tough choices. I had to be creative when I didn't have money for essential items. I was standing in the supermarket looking at the shampoo and soap. I remembered the time I washed my hair with a bar of soap and the filmy residue left behind, so I put a bottle of shampoo in my cart. Bathing with shampoo was definitely a better choice. I bought store brand items and used coupons. If I ran out of laundry detergent, I squirted dishwashing liquid into the washing machine. When I ran out of disposable diapers, I used cloth diapers. If I didn't have laundry detergent or dishwashing liquid, I washed the diapers with bleach and hot water. I rinsed them twice so that the bleach wouldn't give the baby a rash. When I ran out of dishwashing liquid, I washed dishes with laundry detergent, shampoo, scouring pads, and even rubbed a bar of soap on the sponge. The soap was the worst, as it left a filmy residue on the dishes like it did in my hair, but it was better than nothing.

I anxiously watched the numbers adding up on the register as the cashier scanned the items. As the price got close to my limit, I scrutinized the items trying to decide which ones I could do without. *Maybe I can mop with laundry detergent and clean the toilet with bleach*, I thought as I eyed the cleansers. Occasionally I'd have to say, "Can you take these off?" as I handed her the ones that didn't make the cut.

The weather continued to warm, and I wanted to take the boys outside, but it was always such an arduous ordeal. I had tried to keep my stroller folded downstairs in the vestibule, but the landlord knocked on my door one day.

"You can't keep that carriage downstairs. It's a fire hazard," he said.

"But it's folded and against the wall. It's not in anyone's way," I answered.

"It's a fire hazard and if I see it there again, I'll have to get rid of it," he warned.

I didn't see how it would obstruct people from getting out during a fire, but I was afraid that he might throw it away, so I had to keep it upstairs. To go out, I would have to drag the stroller down two flights of stairs to the vestibule, climb back up to the apartment, strap the baby into the carrier, and go back down the stairs with the two kids and a diaper bag. I was fearful of falling down the stairs, so I had to go down very slowly and carefully while holding onto the banister. I had Christopher walk behind me to ensure that if he tripped, he wouldn't roll down the entire flight. I rested a few times on my way down. When I finally got to the bottom, I leaned over the stroller, unzipped the carrier and gently dropped the baby into it. Once he was strapped in, I was able to get the stroller down the stoop going backwards. I made sure that it was late in the day when my neighbors would be returning from work soon. If the weather was nice, we'd venture to the park. Sometimes, I'd just sit on the stoop to get some air. When my neighbors returned from work, I'd ask them to help me carry the baby and stroller up. I didn't do this very often, because I didn't want to be a bother.

One time, I needed to go out and get milk but no one in the building was home. It was so challenging to carry the baby down and back up the stairs, so I waited for him to take his nap then I took Christopher with me downstairs. There was a small bodega right around the corner. I only bought a half gallon because the gallon was too heavy to carry. I prayed the whole time down the stairs, around the corner, and back up, *God, please let the baby be okay; don't let him wake up until I get back; please don't let anything happen while I'm out.* I swung the bag of milk up the stairs and dropped it in front of me until I reached it, just as I did with my book bag as a child. My heart was pounding, and I continued to pray. I thought of all the horrible things that could have gone wrong. I thought about the baby choking or a fire breaking out or him waking up and crying while no one was there to answer his cries. I bargained with God and told him that I would never do it again. I told him that I had no choice, and I begged him not to punish him for my desperate choice. When I reached the top of the stairs, I didn't hear anything. I unlocked the door and immediately went into his bedroom. I walked over to the crib and saw my little angel fast asleep. I made sure I saw his chest rising and falling as he breathed. I thanked God for keeping him safe, and I promised myself that I would never leave him alone again. I told Dad that it was difficult to get milk when I ran out. He suggested keeping powdered milk in the house for when I either had no money for milk or for when I couldn't get out. It was a good idea.

As the baby got older and heavier, I was no longer able to use the carrier to get him down the stairs. Most days, I was cooped up in the apartment. I didn't mind on the rainy days, but when sunshine, warm breezes, and the laughter of children traveled through my windows, I felt like life was passing me by. My children and I were inmates, and the stairs were the bars that stood between us and freedom. While carrying out my sentence, the innocence of the children and the sweet smiles on their angelic faces got me through the days. However, melancholy moods returned in the evenings as I reflected on my situation while they slept.

When I had appointments, I'd schedule them early in the morning so that I could ask Diana to help me carry the baby down the stairs to an awaiting car service before she went off to work. Once, I asked her the night before my appointment if she wouldn't mind carrying the baby down the stairs for me in the morning. She said it would be no problem, but the next morning when I knocked on her door, she called her eleven-year-old daughter and asked her to help me. I was annoyed. I wanted to say that I asked for her help, not her daughter's, but I was desperate, and when you're desperate, you can't be choosy. I was at the mercy of others, which made me feel like I wasn't in control. All I could do was walk nervously behind the young girl as she bounced down the stairs with my baby in her arms, hoping she wouldn't drop him.

I walked into the babies' room one day and saw Andrew holding onto the railing of the crib, bouncing up and down saying, "Da, da, da, da." I felt sad that Hector was missing so much. I often thought about how he didn't care about us. He told mutual friends that I moved away and that was why he couldn't see the kids or try to help us financially. If he really wanted to, he could have left money with my mother, who was still living in the same building as his mother. It was a convenient excuse. I believed that he was relieved that we were out of the picture.

As I watched them sleep, I wondered where Hector was and if he was thinking of them. I wished that I had someone to share all the milestones that the kids were reaching. Although I knew it was for the best to keep Hector away, my heart ached. I clapped and cheered for the children alone, as I had no one to share the amazing achievements that are only special to parents. I also felt a deep sense of sadness for them because I knew I was all they had. I hoped that as they grew from babies to little boys and then to teenagers, I would be enough for them. The fear persisted that I would continue to get weaker and wouldn't be able to do for them. I tried to keep that fear buried in the back of my mind. There was no time or room for worrying about that. I had to live in the present and survive each day as it came. Sometimes, I felt like a machine that changed diapers and made bottles all day.

Lydia stopped by to visit one day. She asked me for a drink, so I offered her some juice. As we chatted, I went to the refrigerator and took out a container of juice. I reached for a bottle and filled it. Lydia watched me as I screwed the nipple onto the bottle, expecting me to give it to one of the kids as she waited for her turn to receive a beverage. She was astonished when I handed her the bottle of juice, and she exclaimed, "I outgrew bottles a long time ago." We laughed until tears rolled down our cheeks.

"Why didn't you say anything when you saw me filling the bottle?" I asked.

"I thought you heard one of the kids get up and you were going to give it to them," she answered.

"Good thing you didn't ask to use the bathroom. I might have powdered your butt and put a diaper on you," I joked.

I loved being a mom, but I sometimes thought about my days at KCC and all the friends I once had. My friend Jerry came to mind. I thought about his promise to buy me a bike and teach me how to ride during my quest for a diagnosis.

I was very fond of Jerry, but we were only friends. After I graduated from KCC, we didn't see much of each other. Hector was jealous and wouldn't stand for me having friendships with other guys. On a hot summer night, when Christopher was a few months old, I was riding around with Megan and her boyfriend in his car. We found ourselves in the Midwood section of Brooklyn, where Jerry lived. I got the urge to see him, so I got out of the car and called him on a payphone. I told him that I was married and had a son. I asked if I could stop by and say a quick hello and introduce him to the baby. He was delighted to hear from me. He came over to the car to see the baby, then we spoke for a while.

It had been about two years since that summer night. In that short amount of time, much had happened. There was nothing stopping me from being friends with anyone. I looked up Jerry's number and called him. Again, he was very happy to hear from me. I told him that I didn't have a telephone, but I would give him my address and maybe we could meet and catch up. When we finally met up, it was as if no time had passed. Jerry was Greek and had large amber eyes and brown hair. I felt like he had a way of looking into my soul when I spoke to him. After the kids were asleep, I told him all the gory details of my turmoil-filled marriage. He listened intently but said nothing. I was surprised that he didn't seem moved by the saga. He expressed no emotion, not even a raised brow or a widened eye. I guess I expected some kind of reaction, maybe a gasp or an "I'm sorry you went through that" comment.

"So, what do you think of all this? I just blurted out my worst experiences and you don't seem moved in any way."

"I remember the day you came to visit me when Christopher was an infant. After you told me that you were married, I asked you if you loved him. Your response was, 'Well, I married him, didn't I?' You never said 'Yes, I love him.'"

Jerry and I spent the summer rekindling our friendship. I cooked for him, and he brought fresh fruits and other groceries over. We spent evenings listening to music and talking for hours. He shared stories of his family life that were painful. We reminisced about the trip to Spain we had gone on in college. I didn't have a camera and mentioned that I wished I had taken pictures from the trip to Spain and that I wished I could take photos of the kids before they grew into the next stage. The next time he visited, he gave me copies of the photographs that he had taken of us in Spain. He brought his camera over and took pictures of me and the kids at the park.

Since Jerry had a car, it was so easy to get out and do things. I didn't feel trapped in the house as I did for the first couple months living on the third floor. When I mentioned that I missed going to the beach, he planned a trip and brought his sister along so that she could look after the kids while we swam together. The waves were rough, and the tide kept knocking me back into the water. He picked me up, carried me out, and put me down on the wet sand. He was so accepting of me, my situation, my children, and my condition.

When my wisdom teeth needed to be pulled out, Jerry sat with the kids in the waiting room of the dentist's office. I was worried that it might be too much for him, but he insisted that he could handle it. Andrew sat in his stroller while Jerry kept Christopher occupied.

I needed to get some forms signed to continue receiving WIC (a program for women, infants and children that provided checks for formula, juice, and cereal). Jerry brought me to the clinic and stayed in the car with the kids while I went to get the papers. On my way out, I heard someone call my name. When I turned to see who it was, I saw Megan running toward me. We hadn't spoken since the night we left her apartment. I heard from Dad that she had given birth to a son, and that he was premature. "Are you going to see your nephew or call your sister?" he asked. Dad had forgiven her, but I wasn't ready. "No, she didn't care about her nephews when she threw us out on the street. I hope her baby is okay, but I'm not going to reach out to her," I answered.

Megan approached me like nothing had happened between us.

"Hi."

"Hi," I answered.

"My baby is in the neonatal unit. I'm here visiting him. Do you want to come and see him?" I didn't have the heart to say no. My anger had dissipated.

"Okay," I answered and followed her down a hallway toward another section of the building. He looked so tiny and frail. His head was the size of an orange. He was lying in an incubator, hooked up to tubes and monitors. I looked at Megan and saw sadness and worry on her face as she looked at him through the glass. I knew that she had a lot of anxiety-filled days and sleepless nights ahead of her.

"Wow, he's so tiny. How long will he need to be in here?" I asked.

"I'm not sure. He has to weigh at least five pounds, and his lungs need to be fully developed before we can take him home," she explained.

"I hope he goes home soon." I replied.

"Where are the kids?" she asked.

"They are in the car with Jerry."

"Can I see them?"

"Yes," I answered and headed toward the doors of the clinic.

We walked over to Jerry's car. Megan said hello to him, then looked in the back seat at the boys. Andrew was nine months old and looked enormous compared to her preemie. She smiled and squeezed Andrew's legs.

"Oh my God, he's so big. Look at those chunky legs!" she exclaimed.

"Hi, Christopher," she said, smiling at him. "He got so tall and look at all that hair."

"I know. He hates getting it cut. He screams bloody murder as soon as the barber gets close to him."

"I better go back in," she said.

"Okay, bye, we have to get going too," I said.

"Okay, bye," she answered and headed back toward the hospital. Once again, a child was born in our family and a feud ended.

Jerry and I continued seeing each other throughout the summer. At times, he would get quiet, and I had to coax him into expressing his feelings. During one of our long talks, he revealed that he had feelings for me since our days at KCC and during our trip to Spain (it was a trip organized by the college). During our friendship, I was always in a relationship with someone else and had only seen him as a friend. I started to think that maybe we could be a couple, but he would be going back upstate to school after the summer was over. We talked about how we wouldn't be able to see each other for months at a time. I didn't want to be in another lonely relationship. As the end of summer neared, there was a sense of anxiety building. I told Jerry that I didn't want to be in a relationship. He said that he loved me. I couldn't say that I loved him back. I was broken, depleted, and needy, and I was afraid to love again. I also realized that I needed to be alone. There wasn't anyone who could fix my situation.

Chapter 6

The Road of Single Motherhood

Andrew was turning one in October. I wanted to have a party to celebrate his birthday and my new life. I wanted to make up for the horrible homecoming he had by creating good memories. I invited family and a few close friends. Dad showed up early to drop off the cake he bought at a bakery. He went into the kids' room to say hi to them. Andrew was in his crib, wearing a little suit that Mom had given him. She always bought clothing for their birthdays and snowsuits or coats for Christmas. It was a great help.

"Where are his shoes?" Dad asked as he picked him up.

"He doesn't have any." I answered.

"What? My grandson doesn't have shoes. I'll be right back."

He left with Andrew. When he returned, Andrew was wearing white shoes with bells attached to the shoelaces. I smiled and thought how lucky we were to have my dad in our lives.

For me, the party was a good way to move on, create memories for the kids, and to surround them with family and friends. Although I was still struggling financially, I had a lot to be grateful for.

I tried my best to give them a happy childhood. I wanted them to enjoy the early years of innocence. I made sure that I celebrated every birthday with a party at home for family and close friends. When money was scarce in those first years, I'd ask my sisters and Dad to bring their gifts over before Christmas so there would be presents under the tree for them to open.

When the weather was mild, I took them to the park to play on the slides and swings. In the summers, they rode their bikes in the sprinklers. Dad was always there, taking us to the beach on summer weekends or picking us up and bringing us to his house for barbecues or holidays. He taught them how to ride bikes and how to swim in his pool. When they wanted a video game that I couldn't afford, he'd buy it for them. He was just as awesome as a grandfather as he had been a dad.

Dad suggested that I apply for Social Security Disability. I had tried after my diagnosis, but it was rejected. I decided to try again and was denied once more. This time, I continued to fight and got a Legal Aid lawyer to help me. I was told that I was rejected because Spinal Muscular Atrophy is not listed as one of the diseases that they recognize. My lawyer decided to compare it to ALS, and I won the case. I was so happy to be getting extra money for the kids, but I was even more thrilled that I did not need Dad to pay my utilities anymore. I was finally feeling independent, and once Andrew was able to get up and down the stairs, it became easier for me to get out. I still had to pull myself up, but I didn't have to carry the baby and the stroller.

A year into my separation from Hector, I filed for divorce. I told Tina that I needed someone to serve him with the petition for divorce papers. She offered to do it. I went to my mother-in-law's apartment to give her the papers. Tina handed Hector the papers. He asked, "What is this?" I told him they were divorce papers. He got angry and said, "You want me to sign it? I'll sign it." I responded with, "You don't have to sign them; they will go through unless you file a counter-petition." I knew he wouldn't go through the trouble of getting a lawyer and fighting against the petition.

A year later, I checked my mailbox on my way out with the kids. I sat on the stoop and opened the letters from my lawyer. My final divorce papers were in the envelope. When I read the words "the marriage is dissolved and the woman may take back her maiden name," I got emotional. Although it was what I wanted, I felt sad. I looked at the kids, who were blowing bubbles on the sidewalk, and felt bad for them at first. I reminded myself of how I was protecting them from the influence he might have had on them. They would not grow up seeing violence and anger, nor would they experience neglect. I was protecting them from becoming like him.

During a regular check-up, my neurologist asked me if I ever got depressed. I thought about it and said no. I did have bouts of sadness, but I didn't think it was depression in a clinical sense. He said that it's difficult living with a disability and suggested that I speak to someone who counsels people with disabilities. I thought that maybe it couldn't hurt to talk about my situation, so I made an appointment with a counselor at the clinic. On the first day, I gave him a quick rundown about my situation (living as a single mom and dealing with SMA). We decided to talk about my failed marriage during the next visit.

The day of my second visit, I was on the phone with Mom. I'm not sure how we started talking about blood types, but I mentioned that mine was B positive (I found this out after giving birth to Christopher). Mom responded with, "Really? Are you sure?" I proudly said yes. She went on to tell me what her and my dad's blood types were. I don't remember what they were, but I do remember that she said it was impossible for their blood types to produce a B positive child. I kind of chuckled and said, "Well, maybe I was switched in the hospital after I was born." I said this because there had been a story in the news about a child that needed a blood transfusion and after the parents' blood was tested, they found out that they weren't the biological parents of their child, and after further investigation, they discovered that they had taken the wrong baby home from the hospital.

I don't know what I expected to be said next, but I definitely didn't expect her to say, "Well, there was another baby girl born the same day as you, with the same last name." I was flabbergasted, to say the least. After she inferred that I might have been switched in the hospital, I said, "I have an appointment at the clinic today. I'm going to ask someone if what you are saying about the blood types is true." She replied, "Okay, let me know what you find out."

When I entered the therapist's office I said, "Forget about my marriage; I have something more important that I need to talk about." I told him about the conversation I had with Mom. He said he knew someone that worked at the blood bank, and he could call her to find out if it's true. He picked up the phone and started to dial the number, then he hung up, looked up at me, and asked, "Are you sure you want to know?" I replied with, "Of course, I do. I have to know." He dialed the number, asked about the blood type possibilities, then thanked the person on the other end of the line and hung up. He then informed me that according to the person at the blood bank, it was true that those two blood types could not create a B positive child.

I thought or hoped that he would say that my mother was wrong. I was prepared to march home and tell her that she had been mistaken about the blood type possibilities. I was shocked, confused, and saddened. As the notion that I was no longer who I had thought I was sank in, I said, "So who am I? That means that my father really isn't really my father, and my sisters aren't my sisters, and my grandmother . . . ?" I couldn't finish the sentence. "Are you alright?" he asked. I don't remember anything else about that session. I just remember having an urgent feeling of wanting to leave. "I have to go. I have to call my mother," I said as I headed for the door.

When I arrived home, I sent the babysitter home and peeked into the kids' room. They were playing on the floor. I walked over to the phone on the kitchen wall to call Mom. I didn't know what to expect or what I wanted her to say. I picked up the receiver and dialed her number. I was shaking as I heard the line ringing.

"Hello," she answered.

"Hi. I just got back from my appointment. I asked about the blood types."

"Oh yeah? What did they say?" she asked calmly.

"They said it's true. Those blood types cannot create a B positive child."

"I knew it. I just knew it. We are so different," she replied, sounding relieved.

As my eyes brimmed with tears, I said, "You're probably glad that I'm not your real daughter, and now you can find out who your real daughter is."

"Oh no, no; you are the daughter I brought home and raised."

I felt dejected that my identity was torn away, but even sadder that it seemed to make her happy. I would have thought that she would be upset or emotional about such a traumatic occurrence. I thought of the families on the news whose lives had been torn apart and how they were planning to sue the hospital for gross negligence. The fact that she seemed to be okay with the situation was heart-wrenching. Was the relief that I wasn't related to her so great that she didn't care who her biological daughter was? I wasn't thinking about a biological family, because I was mourning the loss of the family that I had been raised in. I held the phone to my ear and listened to the unsettling silence while tears of heartbreak flooded down my face. I was dumb with astonishment.

"I have to go."

"Okay, bye," she answered in a cheerful voice.

After I hung up, I called my sister Mary.

"Hello?"

"Hi, Mary," I answered sobbing.

"What's the matter?"

"I'm not your sister."

"What are you talking about?"

"Mom said that I can't be her daughter because my blood type couldn't come from her and Dad's blood type and that there was a baby girl born the same day as me, with the same last name," I blurted out between sobs.

"What? That's not true. It can't be. We *are* sisters. We have the same hair, eyes, and skin; we are both hairy. We both have a mustache"—a feature we both hated—"What is your blood type?"

"B positive."

"I'm B positive, too.

"Are you sure?" I asked. My voice perked up.

"Yes."

"Let me go. I have to call Mom. I'll call you back later."

"Okay, bye."

I called Mom to share my newly found evidence. I was eager to disappoint her with the news that I was indeed her daughter. I wanted to hurt her with the truth as she had hurt me with a falsehood.

"Hello?" Mom answered with the same cheeriness in her voice.

"Hi. I just got off the phone with Mary."

"Oh, yeah?"

"Yeah, and guess what she told me?"

"What?"

"She said that she is B positive also."

"Oh, she is." The cheeriness in her voice had dissolved and was replaced with a solemn tone.

"Yes, so unless both of your daughters were switched in the hospital, I guess I am your daughter," I said with a sort of chuckle, knowing that the probability of that was close to zero.

"Oh no, no, Mary is definitely my daughter. We are so alike. Your father must have told me the wrong information about his blood type." I held the phone in silence for a few seconds then said, "I have to go," and hung up.

Once my sister informed me that we both had the same blood type, my identity was instantly restored, but I then carried a scar that will always remind me that Mom's denial ran so deep that she tried to find another way to reject me or not believe that she has a daughter with a defect. It hurt when she threw me out of the apartment, but this time she tried to throw me out of the family. I didn't talk to Mom for a few months after that. There would be many lapses in our relationship over the years.

Years later, Mary, Mom, Dad, and I all did ancestry DNA tests. The tests revealed what Mary and I thought all along, I was indeed, their daughter.

I tried to compartmentalize aspects of my relationship with my mother. I still wanted to be close to her. She was smart and had good advice, and she was generous with the kids. She bought them a bedroom set when I mentioned that Andrew was outgrowing his crib. She showed up with household items she thought I might need without me ever asking.

Although we didn't talk about SMA, it continued to be a wedge between us. I didn't discuss my physical challenges with her because she often told me stories of people skiing down mountains with only one leg, how people had gotten better after being in terrible accidents, or how someone with MS regained the ability to walk after losing it. I knew there was an underlying message hidden within her stories of triumph. The message was loud and clear: I could overcome my disability if only I tried harder. This theory was not a misunderstanding on my part, because there have been statements that back it up. "She is the way she is because she wants to be that way," something Mom told Megan. A friend of mine bumped into Mom and asked how I was doing physically. Her response was, "She is lazy. She doesn't dance like she did when she was younger." It was a familiar song that had been burned into my memory, and the chorus was, "There's nothing wrong with you; you just want attention."

Life was getting a little easier as the children became more independent. I wanted to be a role model they could be proud of, and I needed to become a better provider. So, I decided to go back to college. I must admit that somewhere in my subconscious, I was also probably still chasing the approval of my mother.

With the kids in school—Christopher in kindergarten and Andrew in pre-K—I enrolled at Brooklyn College in the spring of 1990. My greatest challenge would be transportation, but thanks to Vocational and Educational Services for Individuals with Disabilities (VESID), I was able to pursue my education. VESID provided me with transportation via car service. I expected to be picked up by a regular car service, but the cars that delivered me to and from school were black luxury Lincoln Town Cars.

As I stood in front of the college waiting for my ride, people would stare at me when I got into the fancy cars. One classmate asked me if my father owned the company; another asked if I had a rich boyfriend. I just smiled and shook my head no. I found it amusing that I was viewed as being rich or lucky by strangers. I did feel like a VIP being driven around in those cars, but mostly it was a way to get around safely and with dignity.

I had spent the last five years reading nursery rhymes, singing lullabies, and listening to childish jargon all day. Not that I hadn't enjoyed it, but it was time to add textbooks, lectures, and stimulating conversation to my life. My love for learning was rekindled as I felt a sense of achievement. I was working toward improving my life, and for the first time in a long while, I was able to do something outside of the home that didn't involve the kids. My self-esteem was boosted. I was in control of my situation and was happy to be doing something to better our lives.

I was thinking about becoming a special education teacher, based on my experience volunteering at United Cerebral Palsy as a teenager. I knew it would be a rewarding career. I spoke to Mom about my plans, and she suggested that I consider speech therapy. Mom worked in the school system as a social worker and informed me that if I worked as a school-based speech therapist, I would see students in individual and small group settings. It sounded interesting, so I went to the Department of Speech Pathology and inquired about the program. After speaking to an advisor, I decided to declare my major in Speech and Language Pathology. I was happy that I would still be working with children with various disabilities.

Most of my classes were in Boylan Hall. There was a ramp on the right side of the steps. I had to walk past the stairs and up the length of the ramp before getting to the entrance, but that was much easier and less embarrassing than pulling myself up the stairs. I tried to arrive thirty minutes before class to give myself enough time to walk slowly and rest when necessary. The ramp was steep. I walked slowly and rested every few feet or so. One spring day, I was halfway up the ramp leaning against the railing. There were many students standing about talking. Some were on the steps, some on the ramp, and others standing in front of the ramp. As I moved away from the railing and started to walk up the ramp, I found myself on my knees. There was a young man standing on the side of the ramp talking to a friend. As soon as he saw me fall, he rushed over and picked me up, asking me if I was alright. Embarrassed, I answered, "Yes, I have a bad knee, and it gives out sometimes." He answered, "I have a bad knee also. You shouldn't use the ramp. The stairs are better." I thanked him and proceeded up the rest of the ramp and into the building, careful not to make eye contact with anyone. Although I knew that SMA caused me to fall, I still felt that I had to lie and make up a story like I did when I was a kid. Sometimes it was because it was just easier than the truth; other times it was because I was ashamed of the truth. I felt that it was more acceptable to have an injury than a disease. I was ashamed of the permanence of it, because I didn't want anyone feeling sorry for me.

During my first year back at school, I saw a "For Rent" sign on a building complex a couple of avenues down from my apartment. I inquired about it and was offered a first-floor garden apartment in a building directly across the street from the park where my children often played. It was near the Belt Parkway, which ran parallel to the ocean. The apartment had one good-sized bedroom, a large living/dining room, and a small kitchen. It had hardwood floors and lots of natural light pouring in from the windows. Although it only had one bedroom, I liked that it was move-in ready and, most importantly, it was on the first floor. I would only have to walk up three steps. I loved that it was right across from the park for the kids, but it was three avenues from their school. I would have to walk more but climb less. I gave the boys the bedroom and slept on the sofa. Later, I got a daybed and converted the dining area into a small bedroom for me.

I enjoyed the freedom of just going up a few steps. I was no longer bothered by the stress of anticipating the climb of those horrid stairs as I approached home each day. However, the one block and three long avenues to the kids' school was a killer. I would leave early to give myself time to rest. If it was very cold and my legs were stiff and sore, I would walk them to the corner of the school and watch them run down the block until I saw them enter the building. If snow or ice covered the ground, I walked over one street and watched them until they got to the corner where the crossing guard was. I felt guilty not walking them all the way. I lived in a good neighborhood and knew that once they passed the crossing guard they would be accompanied by other students and parents, but I still felt terrible that I didn't take them all the way to the door. On my way back, I prayed to God, asking him to keep them safe. Occasionally a neighbor would give us a ride to the school or offer to walk with them. I sometimes felt inadequate because I couldn't perform my duties as a mom.

If I had an early class, I'd ask my driver to drop the kids off at their school on our way to the college. Some of them didn't mind, but there were the nasty ones that said it would be a two-stop ride, and they weren't getting paid for that. It was a two-minute ride by car to stop in front of their school and let them out. It wasn't even out of the way. "Come on, it's just three blocks away," I pleaded.

Sometimes I'd get a driver who asked to be my steady driver. This was great, because I'd give them my schedule, and I wouldn't have to call them. It was convenient and saved me the time of looking for a payphone to call them and then waiting until they arrived.

I had no idea of the challenges that were ahead of me. During my first semester, both of my kids contracted chickenpox, and to make things worse, my mother informed me that I had never had it as a child. Right before midterms, I started getting symptoms. Between caring for the kids and myself, I was unable to attend classes and missed some important information. I tried to get notes from a classmate, but with two anatomy classes, you really must get the information firsthand. I didn't do so well that semester, but I trudged on. During that same year, Andrew was diagnosed with asthma and continued to experience chronic ear infections. I was constantly running to the emergency room with him, sometimes for asthma, sometimes for ear infections, and sometimes for both.

One morning during finals week, I noticed that Andrew wasn't feeling well. He didn't have a fever, so I decided to take him with me to class while I took the exam. I planned to take him straight to the doctor after the final. I sat him next to me, handed him some crayons and paper and began taking the exam. Halfway through it, he started moaning and complaining. I reached over and touched him. He felt warm and I realized that he was starting to get a fever. I didn't know what to do. I was in the middle of the exam, but he was getting worse as time went on. My professor approached me and said, "He is obviously not feeling well." I said, "I know, I thought that I would be able to take the exam and then take him to the doctor, but he is getting worse. What would happen if I left?" I asked.

"I will tear your exam up and give you an incomplete in the course. You will be able to make it up within the next six months." I handed her my paper and felt my eyes well up as I listened to the sound of my test being torn. I felt like I was failing as a mother and a student. I gathered my things and my son and headed off to the emergency room.

The doctor diagnosed Andrew with bilateral otitis media (double ear infections) and asthma. No wonder he was so uncomfortable. I felt worse when I realized how sick he was. I missed the rest of my finals that week. I had a paper due in one of my education classes. I wrote a letter to the professor explaining why I was unable to turn it in on time but promised to deliver it to her office in a couple of days. I also stated that I could bring in any doctor's notes to substantiate my claims if needed and I supplied my phone number in case she needed to speak to me. I was outraged and surprised when I received an F on my transcript for that class. I went straight to the head of the department with my son's doctor's notes. I stated that all my other professors understood and none of them failed me. I also informed them that I did hand in the paper a few days later and that I was carrying an A average in the class. They promised me that they would speak to her.

The following semester, an A appeared on my transcript for that class. During another semester, one of my professors threatened that my absences would affect my grade because I was over the allotted amount. I had the emergency room give me a printout of every time I was there with Andrew. He still was unsympathetic and gave me a C.

It was very challenging being a single parent and a college student. When the other students were home studying, I was running to doctor's appointments, parent-teacher conferences, helping my kids with homework, spelling tests, and projects, plus shopping, making meals, and cleaning, all of which were physically draining due to SMA. I spent many sleepless nights watching over Andrew when he had asthma. I let him sleep with me on those scary nights. It was heartbreaking to watch his little body struggling to breathe. I watched his chest rising so very high, and I listened to the wheezing as he labored to breathe. I also felt helpless when he screamed in pain from the frequent ear infections. There were times when I did well, and there were times when I didn't do so well. I kept pushing myself because quitting wasn't an option.

I went into the kids' room one morning to wake them and noticed that one of Andrew's ears was red and was protruding away from his head. I knew that I had to rush him to the hospital, so I got Christopher ready for school and called a car service.

"It's not fair that he gets to stay home from school. He always gets to stay home with you," complained Christopher.

"I know he gets to stay home a lot but he's sick. We are going to the hospital. We aren't having fun." The car service arrived, and we all got in.

"I never get to stay home; it's not fair," he protested.

"I promise that when he gets better, I'll let you stay home one day when he is in school. It will be just you and me, okay?"

"Okay," he said as he reluctantly got out of the cab. I watched until he walked into the school building, then headed to the hospital.

At the emergency room, I was informed that the ear infection that he had been on antibiotics for led to mastoiditis (when a chronic ear infection spreads to the large bone behind the ear}. I was also told that if not treated, it could progress into meningitis. Andrew was admitted to the hospital for a few days. I stayed in the hospital with him all day and slept there during the nights. I only went home to shower. One of my girlfriends had a son in Christopher's class. She offered to watch him overnight and bring him to school for me. Christopher didn't mind because he was having fun playing with his classmate. I did let Christopher stay home with me once Andrew was well enough to return to school. I took him to McDonald's, then drove around looking at all the Christmas lights on the homes in the neighborhood.

Christopher didn't have the health issues that Andrew did. Although he didn't get sick, he had a couple of accidents. The first was when he broke his arm playing football in the park with some friends. His arm was not only fractured, but the bone was displaced, requiring screws to keep the bone in place. The surgery only kept him in the hospital overnight, and like with Andrew, I stayed with him the entire time. He was out of school for about six weeks.

Those were tough years; a time I wished they had a father to help me. I was tired and overwhelmed, but I was also driven. I was determined to get my degree. SMA never let up; it was always there like a thorn in my side, causing anxiety every time I was faced with stairs. I had to fight its ability to break my spirit whenever I fell and find ways to combat the feelings of inadequacy every time, I struggled to walk down the long avenues to take the kids to school. I needed to trudge on when muscle fatigue set in while walking home from the supermarket. It was essential to motivate myself when I feared the dreaded snow, ice, and wind that had the ability to cast me to the ground.

One day after walking them to school, I slipped on snow right near the entrance to the building. I saw a neighbor entering the next building. I noticed that he saw me but kept walking.

"Excuse me. Excuse me. Can you please help me up? I have a bad knee and it's hard for me to get up once I fall," I lied.

He came over and lifted me off the ground. I knew he helped me begrudgingly, but that didn't matter. I was glad to be up on my feet.

"Thank you. Thank you so much."

"No problem," he said.

When I walked with the kids, I tried not to let them know how vulnerable I was feeling. I wanted them to look up to me and to feel safe. I was their protector and had to be strong. It is difficult to feel strong and in control when you fall in front of your children. When I fell in the house, I could crawl over to a piece of furniture and pull myself up, but outside, I was helpless.

One of the buildings in my complex had a few coin-operated washers and dryers in the basement. I would wash at home, then put the wet clothing in the shopping cart and wheel them to the dryers. One day on our way to the laundry room, I fell. I was out in the open with nothing to pull myself up with and no one around to help me. Christopher was nine years old, and Andrew was seven.

I looked at Christopher and said, "You must help me up, Chris. Go behind me and put your arms underneath mine. Use all your strength to pull me up. You are strong; I know that you can do it." He followed my instructions and was able to pick me up.

"Thanks, Christopher. I knew you could do it. You are so strong," I praised him. From that day on, Christopher would pick me up whenever I fell in front of him. I went from being the one that picked my son up and kissed his boo-boos to depending on him to be strong and pick me up. It's not a normal occurrence for a parent to depend on a child in this way. It isn't easy to be in a circumstance where you are vulnerable and helpless in front of your young children. I tried to keep walking and forget that it happened, but there were times that just moving on was more difficult than others. I always kept going, but when the day was over and I replayed the events of the day in my head, moments of gloom would sometimes creep into my thoughts. I tried hard not to dwell on the negative effects of SMA. Although I tried to focus on all the things that I was able to do, there were times when I felt like I was being held back from being the person that I wanted to be.

I worried about getting weaker, and I hoped the weakness would continue to progress at a slow rate. I hated my body for not working the way it should. I sometimes felt like the weight of the world was on my shoulders. I was physically exhausted and emotionally drained. Occasionally, I would get depressed and cry myself to sleep, wishing that I would never wake up. After imagining my kids being alone in the world, I would break out of my pity session. I knew that no one else would care for and love them as I did, so I trekked on, literally dragging myself through the difficult days. My children inspired me to be strong and to keep going. Their needs were primary and did not allow me to wallow in self-pity for too long. Despite my weakness, I had to show them strength. I had to be enough for them.

I know they felt the void of not having a father. Once, I was in my neighbor Diana's apartment with the boys. When her husband came home, her son ran over to him yelling "Daddy." Christopher was about three at the time. He ran over and yelled "Daddy" also. Her husband replied with, "I'm not your dad, kid." I cannot explain the feeling of heartbreak that I felt at that moment. Another time he hugged his uncle and called him "Daddy." Hector's brother hugged him back with tears in his eyes.

One day I had a friend over for dinner and Christopher blurted out, "Mom, why can't he be our dad?" I was embarrassed and changed the subject. Christopher was more vocal about it than Andrew. I suppose he had memories of having a dad around and felt the loss more. When he was in pre-K, his teacher approached me and informed me that the children would be making Father's Day gifts, and she wanted to know if there was someone that he could make his gift for. The teacher was very thoughtful and didn't want to upset him, so I told her that he could make a gift for his grandfather. Christopher came home with a rock with a painted nose and wiggly eyes glued onto it. He happily gave my dad the paperweight. It became a tradition for the boys to make cards and gifts for their grandfather every year. Although he was a suitable replacement, there was still a noticeable void in our family.

When Chris was in the second grade, his school implemented a program called Family Living. Its purpose was to teach the children about different family situations. They wanted to include children from single-parent homes as well as families with two moms and two dads, foster families, children being raised by grandparents, and other untraditional family units. One of the first assignments was for the children to draw a family tree. Chris' tree had four stick figures on it: one of me with long hair and the word "mom" above my head, one of himself with his name over his head, another with "Andrew" written over his head, and one of a man, and over it he wrote "My dad is ded." My heart broke when I read it. I asked him why he wrote that his dad is dead. He answered with, "Well, he must be. I don't see him." I didn't know what to say. I couldn't say he isn't dead; he just doesn't care about you. So, I lied. I said, "I don't know where he is. We broke up and he moved far away to Puerto Rico, and we lost contact with each other." In that moment I knew what Nanny must have felt when I asked her what was wrong with my legs; like her, I created a story that would give him something to tell himself or to tell others when they asked.

One year, I asked him what he wanted for Christmas, and he answered, "I want a dad for Christmas." It took all my strength not to cry in front of him. I felt like it was my fault that he was suffering. My earlier mistake would forever impact his life. I told him that maybe one day we would find a good man to be his dad.

While I was trying my best to raise the boys, I heard that Hector was in jail. He got caught stealing from someone's home. I assumed it was for drug money. While in jail he got clean and, like many inmates, realized his wrongdoings and wanted to repent. He told his sisters that he wanted to see the kids when he got out. The boys didn't know him, and I was afraid that he might be the same person I knew when he got out. An order of protection was issued to me as part of the divorce. It would last until my youngest child turned eighteen. I didn't feel threatened by him anymore, but I didn't want to be the reason the boys didn't know their father. Hector and I began communicating through letters. He wrote about all the wrong he had done and how badly he felt about not being in the boys' lives (sound familiar?). To make sure he was serious, I told Hector that the only way he could see them was if he got court-appointed child visitation.

When Hector got out of jail, he filed a petition for visitation. We went to court, and he was awarded visitation. I sat the boys down and said that their dad had contacted me and wanted to see them. I asked them if they wanted to meet him. They both agreed and seemed excited.

Hector was charming and friendly the day they first met. Andrew had psoriasis which caused his hands to be red, dry, and peeling. I noticed that he was hiding his hands from Hector. I asked why and Andrew said, "What if he doesn't like my hands?" I told Hector about Andrew's concerns. Hector walked over and looked at his hands then kissed them. The boys showed him their room, then I suggested that they all go to the park together. Hector visited the boys every other weekend. He was living in a furnished room and brought the boys to see it. If Hector stated that he didn't have money, I encouraged him to see the kids anyway. "You can take them to the park or play video games with them in their room." I suggested. Once I gave him money to take them to the movies.

I became concerned when Hector said that he was going to be such a good father that I would fall in love with him again. I let him know that it was not a package deal. He was there for the boys, and I was not going to get back together with him. One time he came over to visit and I walked out saying, "Have fun, I have a date." Eventually he stopped coming around to see the kids. Not too long after, I heard that he was living with a woman. That's when I realized that the whole thing was a con. He was hoping that he could get back with me, so he'd have a place to live and someone to mooch off. I felt bad for the boys, but no one can ever say that I kept him from them. They saw for themselves who he was. They would no longer wonder or fantasize about who their dad was.

A couple of months later Hector called me from jail. He wanted me to write a letter on his behalf stating that he takes care of his kids, and they need him. My response was, "Why would I lie?" He answered with, "Because I don't belong in here." I said that I wouldn't write a letter because he stopped seeing the kids after injecting himself into their lives. I told him not to call me again and hung up. I later found out that he had been arrested because he hit the woman he was living with. I never spoke to or saw Hector again.

In the meantime, I had to do everything in my power to take care of my boys. I realized that if I had a car, my life would have less anxiety. In the past, I had shied away from getting my license because I knew that I wouldn't be able to afford a car, insurance, and the maintenance it might need. I came to realize that driving would be vital for when I started working. Once again VESID was there to help. They paid for my driving lessons, since it was a prerequisite for me to become independent.

Dad brought me to the motor vehicle department and kept an eye on the kids while I took the written test for my permit. After a couple of months of practicing, my instructor told me that I was ready for the road test. I passed and received my driver's license. Although I didn't have the money for a car, I would borrow Dad's car whenever I needed to do errands.

Chapter 7
Ceremonies of Passage

It was a warm, sunny day in June of 1994. I was wearing white strappy shoes and a white dress under my red graduation robe. A breeze blew my hair into my face as Dad photographed me standing in front of my apartment building. Christopher and Andrew (ages nine and seven) piled into the back of Dad's car. Before heading over to Brooklyn College, we stopped at Nanny's apartment building. I watched Nanny and Mom exit the building. Nanny had been battling cancer and was pale and weak but walked with a smile and her head held high. I was grateful that she was well enough to attend. Being an immigrant with only an elementary-level education made her especially proud of my accomplishment. She was also proud to see me following in my mother's footsteps as a second-generation college graduate. I was thankful that my parents would be attending together.

Once we arrived at the college, Dad dropped them off at the front entrance, then took me around to the back where the graduates were lining up. I got out of the car and followed the others in matching robes like lost sheep. I bumped into a woman whose name escapes me. She was in one of my anatomy/physiology classes. She seemed just as excited as I to see someone she knew. We were ushered onto the lawn of the campus where rows of white plastic folding chairs awaited. We walked across the turf, our footsteps eliciting the sweet fragrance of freshly cut grass. After we were seated, we listened to long speeches. "Getting a degree is a big sacrifice. You all had to give up time with family and friends to study . . . " As I sat there, I began thinking about all the challenges I had endured.

When the speeches were over, we were told to stand and move the tassels on our caps from the right side to the left. I heard the cheers from the graduates and the applause of the spectators. Above me, a flock of red caps soared in the air. My classmate and I hugged, then said goodbye as we proudly walked through the crowd, looking for our families. When I found my family, my parents were sitting next to each other chatting about people they had known (who had divorced, who had died, and who had taken ill). I stood before them and cleared my throat to get them to look at me.

It was nice to see them talking and being cordial with each other. Mom never attended any of the kids' birthday parties to avoid being near Dad, so I was pleasantly surprised by her behavior. Nanny, Mom, the boys, and I posed for a picture. It depicted the four generations that had come to be because of Nanny's decision to move to America for a better life. Afterward, we celebrated by going out to eat at a restaurant in Sheepshead Bay.

That summer, Mom asked me to visit with Nanny on the weekends while she went to her house in Pennsylvania. I'd borrow dad's car and take Nanny to her favorite spot in Sheepshead Bay. We'd get a bite to eat and sit on benches overlooking the water. Sometimes I'd take her to the park across the street from me. We sat on a bench and watched the boys running around. I also took her to a few of her chemotherapy and radiation appointments. I was honored to walk with my Nanny and let her hold onto my arm just as she let me hold hers when I was weary from walking as a kid. We both walked slowly, but for the first time in my life, I was stronger than she was. If I couldn't borrow Dad's car, we took a cab. On the way back from one of her appointments, I asked her if she wanted me to walk her into the building before heading back to my neighborhood.

"No, honey, I can do it," she answered.

"Are you sure, Nanny?"

"Yes, I'm sure."

"Okay, I'll wait here until you are inside the building." She paid the driver then turned to me and said, "Here, take this," handing me some money.

"No, Nanny, I don't want you to pay me. You were always there for me when I was sick. I am happy to help you now."

"Can you wait until she gets inside?" I asked the driver. I watched her until she entered the building, then turned to the driver. "Okay, thanks," I said, then gave him my address.

The driver, an immigrant from the Middle East, looked at me in his rearview mirror. "That was so beautiful, what you said to your Nanny about wanting to help her because she was good to you when you were little. Many young people don't appreciate their grandparents." I smiled at him, then was saddened by the thought of losing her.

By the end of the summer, Nanny's condition had worsened. She was using a wheelchair in her apartment. I came to see her while the kids were in school. Fluid was oozing from her legs and feet. I got a towel and bent down to dry them. She looked up at me.

"If I'm going to die, at least I tried to live a good life."

"Don't say that, Nanny." When she looked at me, there was sadness and a sort of searching in her eyes that told me that she knew the end was near. I wished I had words to say to make her feel better, but my eyes were mirrors reflecting her concerns back at her.

About a couple of weeks later, Mom called. "I think Nanny is going to die very soon." My sisters and I rushed over to her bedside. When I went into the room, she was on her back, trying to move to her right. She was unable to talk; she was trying to say something but all that came out were moans. It broke my heart to see her like that. We all sat in her living room taking turns going in to comfort her. I went in and stroked her hair back and whispered in her ear, "I love you, Nanny; you are the best grandmother in the world. Thank you for helping me find out what was wrong with my legs." She let out a sound as if she understood what I said. My sisters went in and told her that they loved her also. We stayed until we had to go home to our kids. The next day, we returned. She was no longer trying to move or make sounds. She looked different from the day before. Death was near. Her face was thin and drawn back. Her mouth was ajar, and her cheeks were sunken in. Mom was at her bedside.

"Mom, don't fight it; you can let go," she told Nanny. My sisters and I spewed tears as we watched. Again, we sat in her living room among her things, such as the cuckoo clock brought over from Germany by her cousin who served in the army and her grandfather clock, left to her by an old friend, Pauline, who Nanny took care of during her final days. At noon, the cuckoo cooed twelve times, then a miniature couple appeared through a set of tiny doors. As they spun around to a tune, I thought of all the times they performed for us as children. A few moments later her grandfather clock began to bong. The sound of the clock tolling was a reminder that Nanny's time was running out.

There was a story or a memory behind each of her treasures. I recalled peering into her china closet at the souvenirs family and friends brought her from all over. I loved playing with her miniature tea set made of porcelain trimmed in gold. I could tell she was reluctant to let me play with it because of the worried look on her face when she handed it to us and the way she quickly locked it away after we played with it for a few minutes.

Mary confessed that when she was a teenager, Nanny hid cigarettes for her in the shoe rack that hung on the inside of her closet door. Megan shared that Nanny bought her a bike when she mentioned that she wanted one. We were still receiving birthday cards with money in them, even though we were grown with children of our own. I felt sad when I realized that this would be the first year that I wouldn't get a card from her. It wasn't about the twenty or fifty dollars in the card. I felt special opening up the mail and seeing that she remembered and cared enough to still send cards. With Nanny gone, I would no longer be someone's granddaughter.

We continued taking turns telling her that we loved her. On my way to the bathroom, I looked in on her and saw her chest rising and falling. On my way out of the bathroom, I looked in at her again from the threshold of the room and waited for her chest to rise again but it didn't. I called to Mom, "Mommy, she stopped breathing!" Mom and my sisters rushed into the room. Mom felt for a pulse and said, "She's gone." We all cried hysterically. "She isn't suffering anymore," Mom said. At that moment the doorbell rang. It was Aunt Colleen. When she walked in, I said, "She died, she just died." My aunt put her head down and shook it.

Nanny's funeral was not my first, but it was the hardest. I broke down at the wake as soon as I saw the casket. It was closed, with a picture of her the way we remembered her on top. Neighbors from the building told us stories of how she gave them money when they lost their jobs or fell on hard times. A man with a Russian accent and tears in his eyes told me that my grandmother was such a good person. Others told us how she brought them food or made them soup when they were sick. Yet another neighbor said that Nanny helped take care of her dying mother. We listened to stories that we hadn't heard before but that all sounded familiar because of who she was and how she lived her life. The stories of her kindness and generosity made us so proud to have had her in our lives.

After the funeral, I helped Mom go through Nanny's things. I found a photograph from my graduation— the one of us with Mom and the boys—in a gold frame on her end table. I also found the program from my graduation ceremony. There was a page number written on top. When I turned to the page, the corner was folded in, and my name was circled. I imagined her taking it out and showing it to her neighbors. I was honored to be her granddaughter and pleased to have made her proud of me. I felt blessed that she was able to share that day with me before she died. It was the best graduation present I could have received. My beautiful grandmother, my greatest supporter and my ally, you will forever live in my heart.

Chapter 8

Career and Love

After graduation, my choices were to go to graduate school or go to work and earn my master's degree while working. What I needed to do for my family was work. I bought a used car from a friend. It was an old jalopy the color of a yellow cab. Its bumpers were covered in stickers. It had a makeshift ski rack on top that was covered with duct tape that flapped in the wind as I drove. The rack and pinion were shot, so it was difficult to turn the wheel when the car was parked. If I was in a tight spot, I had to ask the kids to help me turn the wheel. With all its faults, I was happy to own it. I was untethered with my first set of wheels. Dropping the kids off and picking them up from school was a breeze, and shopping was a pleasure. I was no longer bound by the limitations of SMA. I was now able to do many errands in one day and not feel the strenuous effects on my muscles, and most importantly, I didn't have to worry about falling.

I found out about a temporary position at a junior high school in my area. The speech therapist was going on maternity leave, and they needed someone to fill in for a couple of months. I applied for the position and got it. I was so excited to start working that I didn't stop to think about how I would manage the stairs. I jumped in blindly, not knowing if the stairs would stop me from carrying out my duties. I was relieved to find out that the speech room was on the second floor. I would arrive at work early so that I could go up the stairs slowly before any children were in the building. The students changed classes, so I was able to stay in my room and wait for them to come to me. I only had to climb the stairs once a day and going down was still easy for me to do. It felt great getting my feet wet and getting a taste for what the job was like. I loved working with kids and knew I had made the right career choice.

The following year, one of my former classmates told me that they were always looking for teachers at the district that she worked in, and I could probably get a job there with no problem. Sharon set up an interview with me and the supervisor of speech in Bushwick. A couple of weeks later I was offered a job. I was given a few years to earn my master's, so I didn't have to rush into it right away. I was glad that I had a couple of years to get used to working as a single mom before enrolling in a graduate program.

At first, I was disappointed that I didn't get a position in the district that I lived in. I wanted to be close to home and to the kids, but I was placed in a brand-new, barrier-free elementary school. There were no stairs in front of the building and there were two large elevators on the ground floor right near the main entrance. That was well worth the forty-five-minute drive. I don't know how I would have managed going up the stairs multiple times a day if I had gotten hired in an elementary school in the other school district. I realized that not getting a job in the other district was a blessing in disguise.

I felt at home amongst the Hispanic teachers and children I was servicing. I had a lot of support from my supervisor. She provided all the therapists with materials and was always there to share her abundant knowledge. I loved my job instantly. I was finally fulfilling my lifelong dream.

Working as a single mom brought about different challenges. Since I had to be at work at the same times as the kids, I enrolled them in the breakfast program. I dropped them off early, so I'd be able to get to work on time. Andrew was in the fifth grade, and Chris was starting middle school. I couldn't be home to pick them up after school, so I had them go to the local library and start their homework while I traveled from one end of Brooklyn to the other. VESID continued to support me until I became financially independent. They offered to provide me with cab service to and from work for the first six months.

My lease was going to be up by the end of September, and my landlord advised me that it wasn't going to be renewed because the building was going co-op. I was given until October to move out. I found a first-floor apartment in a private house. I only had to climb the porch steps. The apartment was in a different zone, so I had to transfer the kids into new schools. The elementary school was across the street and the middle school was a few blocks away, which made it easier for the kids.

The apartment had two bedrooms, which meant that I could finally have my own room. The rent was significantly higher, but since I was working, I was able to afford it. We moved into the new apartment in mid-October. It had been ten years since the eviction. I was proud to be working as a professional and renting a two-bedroom apartment without any social services.

In November, Diana invited me to watch the Tyson-Holyfield boxing match at her apartment. She still lived in the Bath Avenue apartment building. Her son, Michael, and my boys had been friends since they were toddlers. I had told the kids that we might go to Diana's to see the fight, but when the day came, I was very tired and didn't feel like driving over there and hiking up all those stairs (the very stairs that I dreaded every day when we lived in that building). I told the kids that I changed my mind and didn't feel like going.

"Please, Ma, please can we go? We want to see Michael," they pleaded. "Okay, okay, we'll go," I promised. When we arrived the kids quickly ran off to Michael's room to play. I peeked into the living room to say hello to her guests. Her brother Arthur, nephew Jorge, and his brother-in-law Ralph were gathered around the television. After saying hello, I went into the kitchen to shoot the breeze with Diana as we waited for the main event to start. Jorge came into the kitchen, and Diana introduced me to him. I remembered Diana telling me about her niece and nephew. Jorge and his sister Maria had lost their mom a few years earlier. I recalled when Diana's sister died and how badly I felt that they had lost their mom so early. I remembered seeing Maria and Jorge at one of Michael's birthday parties. I vaguely remembered how Jorge looked. I examined him as we spoke. He had golden honey-colored skin, green eyes, brown hair, and an athletic build. I asked him if he remembered me from when I lived across the hall. He said he remembered seeing me at one of the birthday parties.

"Jorge has recently separated from his wife," Diana informed me on her way out of the kitchen with a bowl of chips in her hand.

"Oh, I'm sorry to hear that. I've been divorced for about seven years now." Although Jorge and I had seen each other before, we had never spoken. I felt at home being with him. It was like I had run into an old friend and had been catching up. I felt a goodness emanating from him. He was soft-spoken and engaging. We wound up sitting in the kitchen, talking, the entire night. I even gave him some advice. "You shouldn't get involved with someone else too soon. You should just date and not get into anything too serious for a while." When the main fight started, we went into the living room and watched Tyson lose to Holyfield (for the first time).

Before the night was over, I told Arthur that I was going to have a painting party, offering pizza and beer as payment. I asked Jorge if he would also like to help and he agreed.

"Don't forget about the painting party. I'm holding you to your word," I reminded them, when they got ready to leave.

"I definitely want to help. I'm going to Puerto Rico for a few days. I will let you know when I get back. Here's my business card," Jorge said, opening his wallet. He realized that he didn't have any more cards and looked kind of embarrassed.

"That's okay, we can get in touch through Diana," I said. He kissed my cheek and left.

I felt a connection to Jorge immediately and had a strong feeling that I should stay in touch with him. I asked Diana to let me know when he returned.

A couple of weeks later, the boys and I went to pick out a Christmas tree. A friend of mine was in the process of putting it in the stand for me when the phone rang.

"Hello?"

"Hi, it's Jorge."

"Oh, hi! How was your trip?" I asked.

"It was great. I was wondering if you still needed help painting your apartment."

"Oh, well, I'm putting up my tree as we speak. My friend is here helping me get it in the stand. I think I'm going to wait until after the holidays to paint, but I'll let you know when I'm ready."

"Oh, okay," he sounded disappointed.

I didn't want to wait until the holidays were over to see him.

"So, if you ever want to talk or go to a movie or something, let me know," I said surprised at the words that came out of my mouth. When it came to guys, I had always been asked to go places or do things first. I rarely initiated anything, but with him, it felt so natural.

"I don't want to seem forward, but how about tonight?" he answered. I didn't expect him to want to get together so quickly.

"Oh, tonight? Let me call you back later when the tree is up, okay?"

"Okay, sure."

After the tree was up, I called Jorge back and gave him my address. I was excited to see him at my door. I showed him in and gave him a tour of the apartment. The smell of pine filled the living room. I asked him to place the first ornament on the tree, which was decorated only with lights. We listened to Sade and Toni Braxton and talked for hours. During a moment of quiet, he looked into my eyes, brushed my hair behind my ear, and moved in for a kiss. After he left, I felt like a schoolgirl that had just had her first kiss. I replayed it in my head a few times the following day.

A couple of days later he called to ask me if I would go with him to his company's Christmas party, which was to be held at the Marriot Hotel in Manhattan.

One of the drivers that drove me to work via VESID offered to take me to the city when I mentioned my upcoming date. As we drove toward Manhattan, my eyes soaked in the skyline. I always enjoyed how the lights of the buildings illuminated against the evening sky. There was something exciting about the city. The plan was to meet Jorge at his job, then walk over to the Marriot together. As I started to ascend the escalator, I looked up and saw a man looking down at me with an admiring smile. I did a double take and realized it was Jorge. He was wearing a gray suit and looked very handsome. I wore a long black dress that hugged my small frame. Jorge showed me his workspace before we headed out.

The hotel was decked with green wreaths and red and white poinsettias. Towering Christmas trees were on display, adorned with shiny ornaments and sparkling lights. The tables in the banquet room were decorated with gingerbread houses and candy canes. Christmas music played in the background as the employees chatted. As we made our way to our table, Jorge introduced me to some of his coworkers. At first, he introduced me as his friend but then introduced me as his girlfriend. After he realized that it might be presumptuous, he turned to me and said, "Is it all right if I say that you are my girlfriend?" I smiled and nodded yes. After dinner, Jorge asked me if I wanted something from the dessert table. I asked him to surprise me with something. I didn't want to tell him that I was nervous about getting up from the chair, because I was wearing shoes with three-inch heels that made standing up difficult. He returned with strawberries covered in dark and white chocolate. He put the plate in front of me and moved his seat closer to mine and whispered, "You are the most beautiful woman here tonight."

Jorge was employed by an advertising company for Broadway plays. The entertainment at the party consisted of the employees participating in a talent show. There were dancers, singers, and groups doing spoofs of Broadway shows. The founders of the company judged the acts and announced the winner. Jorge debuted in a skit from "Guys and Dolls." I was surprised to see how calm he was. He was a good sport, and I could tell he was liked by his coworkers. After the entertainment was over, the music started, and the dance floor was open. We watched his coworkers dance for a while, then decided to go. I didn't want him to know that it was difficult for me to get up, so I slipped my shoes off under the table to make getting out of the chair easier. Once I was standing, I slipped my feet back into the shoes.

The hotel lobby was crowded with people waiting for cabs. Jorge went outside to hail one, too. It was a frigid night, and through the lobby window, I watched his ears turn bright red while the icy wind whipped around him. Finally, we were in a warm cab on our way toward the Brooklyn Bridge.

On that first night that Jorge visited me, I told him about an experience I had had with a guy who claimed to be separated from his wife but wasn't. On our ride home, Jorge said he had something to show me. He reached into his bag and pulled out separation papers that were drawn up by his lawyer.

"I want you to know that I really am separated and I'm working on getting a divorce. I want you to know that I'm serious about it and I'm serious about being with you," he said. After I glanced at the papers, he put them away. I leaned my head on his shoulder as we crossed into Brooklyn.

After the Christmas party, Jorge and I were inseparable. We saw each other so often that we decided we should try to take it slow and only see each other on weekends. Then we decided on weekends and once during the week. We were constantly breaking the rules before we decided to forget them and just follow our hearts.

After the six months of car service from VESID was up, I started driving to work in my jalopy. I was driving home on a snowy day in January. Every time I hit the brakes; the car slid into the next lane. Although I was driving slowly and carefully, I kept on drifting. I was terrified that I would crash into another vehicle. I prayed all the way home. After that scary ordeal, I knew that I would have to buy a new car.

In February, I went to the dealership to look for a new car. I wanted something new with a warranty because I didn't want to worry about it breaking down. I went to a Chevy dealership and got a loan for a brand-new, green 1997 Chevy Cavalier. It wasn't a luxury car but compared to the wreck I was driving—it was luxurious to me. I felt safe with its new tires and a three-year warranty. The kids came with me when I picked up our new car. The salesman gave me a bottle of champagne to congratulate me on buying my first new car. The kids were excited and proud. There was a commercial on television at the time that showed someone getting a new car. The salesperson said something to the effect of, ". . . Congratulations on getting your first new car," then in slow motion, they handed the keys to the new owner. Christopher took the keys and reenacted the commercial, saying, "Congratulations on buying your first new car." We all laughed and eagerly piled into the car and headed home.

Having a job made life so much easier. Besides buying a car, I was able to buy food without using food stamps, and I no longer had to go to the clinic. The kids were now able to have a private doctor.

Things were falling into place, but SMA continued to show its ugly face. One cold winter's day I went grocery shopping with Andrew after work while Chris stayed at home. I parked the car and started walking down the block toward the house when I fell on my knees with the shopping bag handles still wrapped around my hands. I couldn't get up, and Andrew was unable to help. I asked him to run into the house and get Chris. I remained on my knees in the street until he came to help. A neighbor passing by asked me if I was all right. I nodded my head and looked away so that she would move on because I knew she wouldn't be able to help me. A few moments later the boys came running toward me. Chris picked me up and they both carried the packages into the house.

SMA was cruel and heartless. There was no place to hide from its wrath. As a speech provider, part of my job was to pick up my students and then return them to their classes after therapy was over. This meant a lot of walking back and forth and up and down every thirty minutes, several times a day. There were times when the students weren't in their classes because schedules had changed. This sent me scurrying about looking for them. Since I needed to use the elevator, this often meant walking around the long way instead of using the stairs that would be closer to their rooms. Sometimes they were on the same floor but many times they were scattered about the building on different floors and different sections of the building.

I fell in the hallways and in my room on many occasions. If I fell in my room, I could crawl over to one of the kids' lower chairs, pull myself onto the chair and then get up from there. If I fell in the hallway, I would need a man to come pick me up. One time, I fell in the hallway, and no one was around. I crawled on my knees to my classroom, opened the door, then crawled over to a chair to pull myself up. I cried in my room that day because I felt broken. I felt like I was pretending to be something that I wasn't. I was pretending to be a professional and a role model for kids. *Who was I kidding? How was I going to pull this off? How long will I last?* I wondered. I looked at the clock and saw that it was time for my next group. I dried my tears, collected myself, and went back out into the hall to fetch my students. I had to move on and not let SMA prohibit me from doing my job.

There were times that I had no warning that I was about to fall. Once, I fell right outside my door. A few seconds later, someone walked into the hallway. I pretended to be fixing the decorations on the door. After the person was out of sight, I opened the door and crawled over to a chair. Another time, I was hanging work on a bulletin board and fell outside another teacher's room. I crawled to her door and opened it. While on my knees with the door cracked open, I asked, "Can I borrow a chair?"

"Sure," she answered. Her para brought a chair over to me and I slid it out into the hallway. It was a very low chair that kindergarteners use. I was able to sit on it, but I couldn't get up off it. My mind raced as I wondered what to do. A few moments later, a male counselor came out of the stairway and started walking toward me.

"Excuse me, can you help me up?" I asked.

"Sure," he answered and walked over, looking concerned.

I extended my arm out to him, and he pulled me up off the chair.

"Thanks, my back went out and I couldn't get up," I lied.

Another time, I walked into a classroom and stepped on a crayon. My foot rolled over it and before I knew it, I was on the floor. Although I tried to be aware of possible culprits, there were things I just couldn't avoid, like the time I was exiting the elevator on my way out at the end of the day. My feet lost traction, and I slipped, landing flat on my back. My feet were like the wheels of a car hydroplaning over a huge puddle. The assistant principal and a teacher rushed over to help me up. I touched the back of my coat, expecting it to feel wet. I would have sworn that someone had spilled water on the floor, but my coat was dry. I looked at the floor and saw a large area covered in glitter. Someone hung up a poster covered in glitter on the wall above the elevators, and a bunch of it had fallen off. Who knew that glitter could be so dangerous?

On a warm spring day, I was walking toward the door to leave, and a student came running out of the auditorium and bumped into me, pushing me onto the floor. He kept running without realizing that he had knocked me down. Thankfully, the custodian walked by soon after and helped me up.

The falls weren't limited to inside the building. On a day after a snowstorm, I exited the building. The snow had turned into ice, but there was a shoveled path that I could walk on to get to my car, parked right in front of the building. I thought I was safe and could make my way to my car without incident, but some children were picking up pieces of ice and throwing them at each other while I stood and talked to a teacher. Without my knowledge, a piece of ice landed near my foot. I stepped on it and lost my balance. The teacher was unable to help me up. Finally, a male parent came over and lifted me off the ground. After every fall, I tried to convince myself that that would be the last one. *I'll try harder to avoid it*, I told myself, but sometimes my legs just gave out because of exhaustion, and other times, for what seemed to be no reason.

People with SMA have what I call weak spells. These are periods of a couple of days or so that we feel extra weak. On these days, the things we are usually able to do are more difficult, and the difficult things are extremely difficult. I tried to stay home and rest on those days, but it wasn't always possible. There were times that I felt so weak that I knew it was dangerous for me to be walking. I literally dragged myself out of bed and into work on many of those days.

I experienced one of those days early on in my career. I left the building after all the parents and children were gone. My muscles were very fatigued. I was struggling to walk and hoping that I would not fall. I trekked out of the building. My car was parked directly across the street. It wasn't far at all, but it felt like it was miles away. I inched toward the curb and held on to a parked car to step down without falling. A truck was stopped at the stop sign and waiting for me to cross. I signaled for him to go but he insisted that I go first. I plodded on. I got close to the truck and held on to its hood for support, but the driver started backing up. I think he was trying to give me space, but that made it worse because then I couldn't hold on to it. I was shifting my weight from one side to the other, limping badly. A young man was looking out the window of the building that faced the school and asked if I was okay. I think I had grimacing pain on my face. I nodded yes, although I wasn't okay at all. I had to stop and rest before making it across the street. I took so long to cross a one-way street. Although each step brought me closer to my destination, it brought a horrifying threat of falling. I finally made it to the car. I signaled for the truck to pass. I leaned against the car and pried the door open. I plopped into the driver's seat and pulled my legs into the car with my hands. Sitting was such a relief. I shut the door and rested for a minute, then drove away with tears in my eyes. I was so scared that I was not going to be able to keep my job. I was afraid that after struggling through college, I wouldn't be able to work in the field that I loved. I felt defeated. SMA was kicking my ass. I told a friend, and she suggested that I use a walker. Without hesitation I replied with, "I'm not using a walker!" That day sticks out in my memory as one of the most physically challenging days at work. I didn't give up. I kept on trying. I fought against the fatigue and the anxiety of falling. I pushed and challenged myself to overcome my limitations, because I was too stubborn to give in and too determined to keep my career.

During the first couple of years of working, there were no signs restricting parking on the street of our school, so parking close by wasn't too difficult. Eventually, the city put up signs restricting parking. This made finding a spot close by more difficult. Walking a block or two was difficult for me. It would only add to the stress of my day. I was fearful of windy days because a strong gust could knock me down, and as always, ice and snow were my enemies. One day, I exited my car, and the wind was so powerful that I had to lean against the car until the gust subsided. I was afraid to move. I looked at the patches of ice on the ground and knew that it was a bad situation. I noticed a teacher coming down the block. I waited until she approached and asked if she wouldn't mind me holding onto her arm because I was afraid that I would slip on the ice. Another time I was parked diagonally across the street on a rainy, windy day. I made it across the street but fell near the gate at the opening of the front yard. After I fell, I looked up and saw a parent volunteer rushing out into the rain to pick me up.

I applied for an on-street handicap parking permit. It was different from the permit that hangs on the rear-view mirror when parking in designated spots at malls or shopping centers. It allowed me to park almost anywhere. I didn't have to obey the alternate side of the street parking regulations or feed the meters if I parked in front of one. I could park in spots designated for different officials like police, doctors, and diplomats. The only places that I couldn't park were in front of bus stops, fire hydrants, and crosswalks.

When I first got the permit, I felt kind of guilty using it. I almost felt like I didn't deserve it, because it made life so easy. It allowed me to park in front of my school every day of the week without getting a ticket. The stress of looking for a spot was over. One day. when I arrived at work, a teacher said, "You are so lucky that you can just pull up at any time before school starts and get a spot. I have to get here an hour early just to find a good spot close to the building." I smiled at her and said, "The lucky ones are the ones that can walk a few blocks to get a spot." She smiled and nodded in agreement. As the years went on, I would find walking into the building difficult, even though I was parked in front. I learned to stay home when winter storms dumped several inches of snow on the city. It was too scary to climb up and over large piles of snow that had been shoveled onto the curb.

It started becoming difficult to get out of my car because the seat was low. Five years after buying my first car, I was ready to trade it in for an SUV. The seat was high, (butt height) which made getting out a breeze, and getting in was easy when I was parked near the curb. I had to tiptoe a little when the car wasn't near the curb, but that wasn't a problem. When the snow piled high against the curb, I could use the four-wheel drive to climb up on the snow and step down on the sidewalk. If it was bad, Jorge would drive me to work, help me in, and then take the train into the city from the station near my school. Once, he had to ask the janitor for a shovel so he could make a spot for me to park. He removed the snow from the curb so I could step onto the sidewalk.

Early on in my career, some people didn't know that I had a disability. Although I tried to hide it, I had a very distinctive gait. My hips dropped from side to side as I walked. My gait was often mistaken for being "sexy." Teachers saw me walking slowly down the hall with my hips "switching." A teacher once said that I walk like a model when I entered her room. I smiled and thought, *I wish that's why I walk this way.* One of my colleagues, who did know I had a disability, told me that her students wanted to know why she didn't walk sexy like me. We both chuckled. Once I was walking from the teacher's lounge toward the elevator. There was a substitute security guard sitting at the desk in front of the elevators watching me as I approached. As I got closer, he said, "You have such a great walk." I guess the fact that I was young, attractive, and dressed nicely added to the whole "you look sexy" idea. I often wondered what people would have thought if I was a man. Some people who didn't know me thought I was stuck up or something. I hadn't realized it until one day when I was decorating a bulletin board and a para walked by. I asked her if she could help me hold the paper while I stapled it. When we were done, I said "Oh, my back is stiff."

"Oh, you have a back problem? I was wondering why you walked like that. I was thinking, damn, she cute, but she doesn't have to flaunt it."

I couldn't help but laugh. Here I am, struggling to walk around the school, hoping not to fall, and someone is thinking that I'm strutting around thinking that I'm cute.

There were other times that my gait told another story. When I was tired or struggling, it showed. Some people were intuitive and asked if I had a back problem. Others asked me if I was in pain, and one even offered to give me some of her pain medication, which I quickly declined. There were the occasional comments from observant children who asked why I walked so slowly or why I walked like "this" as they mimicked me.

During my fourth year of teaching, my supervisor stopped by for a visit when both of the elevators were out of service. After observing my lesson, she walked down to the second floor with me to drop off my students. She witnessed me pulling myself up the stairs on our way back up. I was a little embarrassed for her to see me, but I had no choice. As we were walking down the hallway, I fell. She couldn't help me up, so I sent her into the library to get help from a male para.

A couple of months later, she informed me that due to my disability, I was entitled to have a paraprofessional to assist me. The para would pick the students up for me so that I wouldn't have to do all the legwork involved in gathering groups of children throughout the building. Although I was embarrassed that my supervisor saw me fall, it turned out to be a good thing. I filled out the paperwork for the para and waited for approval.

Chapter 9

Millennial Bride

Jorge and I fell in love quickly, and after six months of dating, we decided to live together. I asked the boys if they would mind if he lived with us, and they eagerly gave their approval. Jorge and I signed a new lease for an apartment building with an elevator and an underground parking garage. Having the parking was such a help. I didn't have to worry about looking for spots or cleaning snow off the car in the winter. We began our lives as a family in June 1997. A couple of weeks after we moved in, Jorge cashed his paycheck and came into our bedroom, where I was resting. He took the money out of an envelope and threw it up in the air. As the bills came raining down over me, he said, "I work for you." Although I was financially independent, it felt good to have someone to share the responsibilities with.

Jorge and I supported each other in raising our children. Millie, Jorge's daughter (age five), gave me an opportunity to experience a mother and daughter relationship. I loved buying her clothes and dressing her up, but most of all, I enjoyed reading to her and helping her with schoolwork.

Jorge and I met ten years after I left Hector. It was worth waiting for the right man to be a father figure for the boys. He brought them to flower shops on Mother's Day and my birthday so they could help pick out flowers for me. In every way that he helped me, he was silently teaching them how to treat a woman. I was so grateful to have him setting a good example. I was proud that my younger self was afraid that Hector would be a detrimental influence on them. She made some tough decisions, and they paid off.

When we first started dating, I explained my limitations and prognosis of SMA to Jorge. I told him that I may lose my ability to walk and asked him if it would bother him to be with someone in a wheelchair. Jorge said that he loved me no matter what the future brought. He did everything he could to make my life easier. When we went somewhere that had steps, he carried me, so I didn't have to struggle. Whenever I fell, he quickly picked me up. He dropped me off and picked me up in front of places if close parking wasn't available. He always brought the car around to the front of our apartment building before I went to work. Once I was safely in the car, he'd kiss me goodbye and walk to the train station. I always held his arm when we walked in the street. I felt safe and protected when I was with him. My anxiety was diminished when he was by my side.

Once we went to the movies and the only seats available were a few levels up. He scooped me up in his arms and carried me to my seat, then went off to get popcorn. As he walked away, the woman sitting next to me said, "Now, that's a man!" Many times, spectators thought that he was being romantic. Although he carried me out of necessity, it was still romantic to me.

Just knowing that I'd see Jorge at the end of even my toughest days made them more bearable. I knew he would be there to listen and truly understand what I was going through. I didn't have to hide or lie about the effects of SMA. I could be totally raw and vulnerable with him.

On December 4, 1999, the day before my thirty-seventh birthday, Jorge brought me to Windows on the World restaurant at the top of the World Trade Center in Manhattan. The food was delicious, the ambiance was romantic, and the views of the skyline were spectacular. After dinner, he ordered some champagne. I looked away for a moment and when I looked back there was a black velvet box on the table in front of me. I looked at him in amazement and said, "Where did you get that from? Let me see! Let me see!" I squealed. He opened the box and revealed a beautiful, round, one-karat diamond ring set in platinum with two baguettes on either side. It sparkled brilliantly as he put it on my finger. He asked me to marry him, but I was so distracted by the ring that I didn't even hear him. I was admiring the ring on my finger when a woman at a table across from us noticed and yelled out, "You two are too cute!" I got embarrassed and whispered to Jorge, "Let's get out of here." We finished our champagne, he paid the bill, and we got up to leave. As we walked away from our table, the woman and the people at her table started to applaud. Everyone around us was watching and clapping as we exited the restaurant. We made our way through the underground garage and found the car. I was sitting in the car looking at my ring.

"I proposed and you never answered me."

"Really?" I said, still beaming with excitement. "Okay, ask me again."

"Will you marry me?"

"Yes, yes, of course I will," I answered then leaned over and kissed him.

When we got home, I rushed over to the boys to show them the ring.

"Look, we got engaged!" I said, showing them the ring.

"Yeah, we know," Andrew said,

"Jorge showed it to us a few weeks ago," Chris chimed in.

"What? You told them?" I asked Jorge.

"Yes. I showed them the ring and asked them if they would mind if I asked you to marry me," he explained. I loved how thoughtful he was.

The next day, Jorge invited a few family members over to celebrate my birthday and announce our engagement. It was such a joyful day for me. It was the happiest birthday I had ever had. The following day, Jorge sent flowers to me at work. The card read, "Thanks for saying yes." The teachers at work were impressed with him. One jokingly asked if he had a brother. I was elated to be engaged, in love, and to start planning my wedding. I wanted to be a millennium bride, so that meant we had less than a year to plan the wedding.

Like most brides, I wanted my wedding day to be perfect. I wanted a traditional church wedding with a reception to follow. Jorge insisted on a Hawaiian honeymoon, so we booked a trip to Maui. In the days before the wedding, I tried not to do too much because I didn't want to do anything to bring on a weak spell. I chose my shoes very carefully. I picked out a pair of white satin shoes with a two-inch stacked heel. I wanted to avoid a high stiletto heal to ensure I wouldn't fall. The shoes were very comfortable and easy to walk in. I even purchased a pair of white satin ballerina flats in case my feet got tired or sore.

Jorge and I wanted our children to be a part of the wedding. We weren't just creating a life for ourselves; we were creating a blended family. My sons were going to be ushers, and Millie would be our flower girl. We bought the kids claddagh rings as a symbol of the union of our family. Our wedding date was set for September 3, 2000.

On the day of the wedding, I woke up to see my wedding countdown calendar flashing on my dresser. Jorge went to his grandmother's apartment to get dressed. I jumped up, and took a shower, then headed over to the hair salon with Millie. The sky was overcast, and the air was thick with heat and humidity. Mom, my sisters, and my niece were at the salon when I arrived with my tiara and veil in hand. Waves of excitement and anxiety rolled over me as I sat in the salon. The stylist washed and set Millie's hair into beautiful ringlets that bounced when she moved. A wreath of small silk flowers was placed on the crown of her head. She smiled and clapped with glee when she saw her reflection in the mirror. My hair was put up with lots of pins and a ton of spray to ensure that it didn't move or frizz in the very humid weather. After Millie and I were done, I drove back to my apartment. My maid of honor arrived soon after to help me and Millie get ready. I was afraid of slipping in my new shoes, so she scuffed up the soles with a file. I was doing everything in my power to prevent a fall. I prayed and asked God to help me get through the day without falling.

Before I knew it, the photographer was knocking on the door. He took pictures of me alone, then with Millie, who looked angelic in her long white dress. I was very proud to memorialize this special event with my sons, who looked very handsome in their tuxedos.

After all the photographs were taken, the bridal party piled into the limo and Mary, my matron of honor, and I got into a Rolls-Royce. Mary hugged me and said she was so happy for me. As we drove to the church, I continued to experience waves of happiness, anxiety, and fear. Questions raced through my mind. *What if I have a hard time going up the steps leading to the alter? Everyone will be watching me. What if the chair is low and I can't get up?* As we arrived in front of the church, the driver's horn honked to the tune of "Here Comes the Bride."

The videographer was there ready to start filming. I had trouble getting out of the car because there was so much room between the seat and the door. After trying a few times, I figured out a way to get up and out. I got on one knee, then lifted the other leg out and onto the ground. My long, flowing gown concealed the maneuvers. Once I was out of the car, I faced the challenge of the steps. Instead of walking up the middle of the steps, I'd have to go to the side where the banister was. It was something I had done many times before, but it wouldn't look graceful. I turned to the videographer and said, "Don't film me going up the stairs." He nodded and said "Okay." I was at the top of the stairs in front of the church doors when the limo drivers rolled out a white runner. Then one of them took the bottom of my train and pulled it up, letting it fan out on the floor behind me. I waited for the bridesmaids, ring bearer and flower girls to make their way down the aisle. I was then instructed to start walking. I held onto Dad's arm, as I had so many times as a kid when I was weary. This time, it was different. I walked slowly and held on to his arm not to help me, but because it was a tradition. I felt lucky and proud to walk with him. He had always been by my side, supporting me. Holding on to him helped calm my anxiety as we slowly made our way down the aisle. My flowers were getting heavy in my hand, so I gently leaned on his arm to help support the weight. I heard someone say, "Her dress is so beautiful." I looked down the aisle and saw Jorge waiting for me, with my sons standing alongside him. I smiled and knew that everything would be all right. The stairs and the chair did not worry me because I knew he would be there for me. When I reached Jorge, Dad removed my veil and kissed me on the cheek. Jorge put out his arm for me to take. I looked at the stairs and whispered, "I need help." Mary held on to one arm and Jorge to the other as I made my way up the few steps. The priest directed us to sit. Mary and I were instructed to sit in chairs on one side while Jorge and his best man had chairs on the other side. I was not sitting next to him and started to worry about how I will get up when the priest directed us to stand. I looked over at Jorge; he smiled and softly said, "You look beautiful," then signaled that he would help me up. When the time came for us to stand, he walked over to my chair and helped me up. I was a little embarrassed, because if he was sitting next to me, it wouldn't be as obvious that he was helping me up. Having to walk over to me made it more obvious. There was nothing I could do; I couldn't hide having SMA. After the gospel was read, the priest told us to sit together, and after observing Jorge helping me up a couple of times, he told us we could stand in front of our chairs until the Mass was over.

    The date of our wedding was six years and one day after the date of my sweet Nanny's death. During the ceremony, Megan and Jorge's sister Maria lit candles in memory of my grandmother and their mother. At the end of the Mass, we said our vows and were pronounced husband and wife. We kissed and faced our family and friends while they applauded. After the ceremony, we posed for pictures in front of the church while the wedding party threw rose petals at us. I was so happy that the ceremony and the stress related to it were over.

    The next step would be going to the studio to take pictures. This would be the least stressful part of the day. As the guests traveled to

Staten Island for the cocktail hour, we headed over to the photography studio.

When we arrived at the studio, the photographers asked for the groom and groomsmen to be photographed first. While I was waiting, I got a glimpse of myself in a full-length mirror. The top of my dress had a sweetheart neckline with off-the-shoulder straps. The bodice was formfitting and embellished with sequins and pearl appliqués that glistened when the light caught them. The skirt of the dress was full and made of tulle with scattered appliques and a satin hem. As I swayed, the dress opened like a blooming flower. It looked lovelier than it had in the dimly lit bridal shop. I had never felt so beautiful in my life. I also felt lucky and blessed because I had met and married my Prince Charming after all the adversity I had endured. He was my knight in shining armor, not because he saved me from life's hardships, but because he chose to walk alongside me during them, making it easier whenever he could.

The bridesmaids and I were called to take group pictures. After the bridal party was photographed, they went on to the reception hall while Jorge and I were photographed alone. The photography studio we'd chosen had a garden in the backyard. There was a bridge overlooking a small pond, an area with pillars that looked like a scene from Italy, a swing with vines wrapped around the ropes, a beautiful fountain, and a Japanese garden with benches. Flowers and foliage surrounded us with every step. It looked like a small paradise.

It was wonderful to hear the photographer say phrases like, "Turn to your wife" and "Look at your husband." I wanted time to slow down so I could enjoy every moment that we were alone. I knew the reception would be fun and that I would be busy greeting and talking to guests as well as eating and taking more pictures, so these moments were just for us.

After we posed in front of the fountain and on the swing, we were led down a stone path toward the bridge. The path was very narrow, so Jorge went on ahead of me. The main photographer was in front of

Jorge and his assistant was behind me. As I followed behind him, my most dreaded fear came true. I stepped on a loose stone, twisted my foot, and fell, fast and hard. I called out to Jorge, and he quickly turned around, and got behind me to lift me up. When he let go of me, I tried to take a step and went down again because the pain was so great. Once I was up the second time, I looked down and saw the broken stone that I had twisted my foot on. I pointed it out to Jorge. The photographer's assistant pointed at another cracked stone and said, "Be careful, there's another one." My foot was very sore. When I tried to put pressure on it, it hurt like hell. I figured that I must have sprained it and tried to walk it off. The pain was so intense that I could no longer continue through the garden; I needed to sit down. They took us into the studio and took some pics of me sitting on a bench and leaning on a piano while I rested my foot. I asked for ice, and they scurried to get some. We chose this photographer because of the beautiful garden. I was determined to finish taking those pictures, so I limped back into the garden. With every step I took, the pain got worse. We got to the bridge, and it was so difficult to climb because it had a curved step. It took a couple of tries, but I finally got on it. I smiled for the camera as if nothing was wrong because I didn't want my pictures to be ruined. As we left the garden Jorge picked me up and carried me over the threshold, through a pair of French doors back into the studio. The photographer said, "Jorge, can you hold her a bit longer? That's a great shot." After he photographed us, Jorge put me down, and we headed out to the Rolls Royce waiting in front of the studio. I kept the ice on my foot as we drove. As long as I didn't put pressure on it, it didn't hurt. I planned to ice it again when we got to the bridal room of the reception hall before dinner. As we sat in the car I could see our reflection in the wide rearview mirror. My dress encompassed the seat and covered one of Jorge's legs. I remember admiring how beautiful we looked. Jorge kissed me and told me that he loved me. I soaked in the moment and enjoyed the ride from Brooklyn across the Verrazzano Bridge into Staten Island.

When we got to the reception hall, the cocktail hour was over. I was told that there was no time to go to the bridal room. It was close to eight o'clock, and we were to be introduced to our family and friends. I had no time to rest or ice my foot. With every step I took, I felt a burning pain. I could hear the music playing and the laughter of my guests through the closed double doors of the reception room. The bridal party and parents were summoned to the hallway to line up. After the bridal party was announced, the doors were closed. When the doors reopened, we were introduced as husband and wife for the first time. The excitement and adrenaline overpowered the pain. Jorge and I entered the room and walked under the arms of our bridal party as our guests looked on. Jorge and I chose "The Power of Love" by Celine Dion for our first dance. Our guests stood and clapped while we danced. I didn't want the pain to prevent me from enjoying the moment. We danced, kissed, and smiled for pictures. After the dance, we were told to be seated at our dais. The dais was elevated by a short flight of five steps. When we approached the staircase, Jorge scooped me up in his arms and carried me up to our table. The guests applauded and hollered, thinking that he was being romantic.

It felt so good to sit down and get off my foot. I tried to change into my ballet flats, but it was more painful to wear them than my shoes. We informed the DJ not to call me to the dance floor. Shortly after sitting down, the maître d' brought me a fresh bag of ice. He climbed under the table to put the bag of ice on my foot. Before our dinner was served, the photographer informed us that it was time to take the family pictures. I dreaded getting up, but I had no choice. We took pictures for about an hour. While we were standing, I put all the pressure on my good foot, allowing the injured one to rest. After each resting period, the pain in my foot increased. When we returned to the reception room, it was time for the father-daughter dance. I danced with my dad to "Daddy's Little Girl." In the absence of his mother, Jorge danced with his grandmother, which brought many to tears. Since I couldn't dance to the fast songs, Jorge and I danced to another slow song. I danced three times that night, and as the night went on, the pain continued to intensify. We cut the cake and did the bouquet and garter toss. Instead of going around to the tables to greet our guest, we had them come up to the dais to congratulate us. I was in pain and unable to fully enjoy myself, but I got pleasure in watching my guests have a good time. Jorge and I smiled as we watched them dancing. At the end of the night, we were getting ready to leave when the videographer asked us to thank our guests on tape. I was in such pain, and I just wanted to leave. I rolled my eyes, and I said, "Okay, let's get this over with." I put on a smile and thanked our guests. I think I could have been nominated for an Academy Award because I was able to hide the grimacing pain. As soon as he shut the camera off, I turned to Jorge and said, "Let's get out of here." I was done. I had gotten through the night and was eager to go home and put my foot up.

When we left the building, a limo was waiting for us. My foot hurt so badly I could barely walk. I couldn't step up to get into the limo. Jorge was busy talking to a guest while I stood by the limo. Christopher grabbed me by the waist and pulled me in across the back seat. By the time we got home, I was unable to put pressure on my foot at all. Jorge had to carry me from the limo to the front door of our building and then into the elevator. Once I was in the elevator I stood on my good foot. When the elevator arrived on our floor, he carried me into the apartment and put me down on the bed.

I hadn't seen how my foot looked. I couldn't wait to take off the dress, shoes, and stockings so I could put my foot up and ice it. With a flight scheduled to depart early the next morning, I was hoping the swelling would go down overnight. Once I got a look at my foot, panic set in. It was black and blue and so swollen that my toes looked like tiny nubs. I realized that I had to go to the emergency room to have it examined. I looked at Jorge and saw sadness in his eyes. I started to cry. I felt horrible about ruining our wedding and possibly missing our honeymoon. I didn't want to lose hope. I expected that they might be able to wrap it up tight and we would still be able to go on our honeymoon. I know how long an emergency visit could be so I called the airport to see if there was another flight we could take if we missed ours. I was given the times of the next two departing flights. I removed the veil but didn't want to waste time and energy pulling all the pins out of my hair. Once again, Jorge had to carry me to the elevator and then from the elevator to the street and then to the car. Once we got to the hospital, he went in to get a wheelchair.

I was wheeled into the emergency room wearing a pair of shorts, a t-shirt, and the tiara with up-do intact. Nurses asked me if I was at a wedding. I answered with, "Yes, mine." I told them how I fell on a cracked rock while I was taking pictures. They were all surprised to hear the story. They said that they had treated guests who had fallen on the dance floor at a wedding, but they had never treated a bride. The doctor ordered an x-ray. As I waited for the results, I was talking to a particularly friendly nurse. I was telling her that I was worried that I would have to cancel my honeymoon. Another nurse came into the waiting area and said, "You aren't going anywhere; your foot is broken." I was devastated. The friendly nurse said, "Don't listen to her. Go on your honeymoon. Girl, you can work around that foot."

I left the hospital with a splint on my foot, crutches, some Vicodin, and a referral to follow up with an orthopedic doctor. I decided to cancel our honeymoon because I didn't think I would have a good time. I'd rather go when my foot was healed and I could enjoy myself. In the morning, I called my travel agent to let her know that I had to cancel the trip and reschedule it. She informed me that since I had insurance it wouldn't be a problem to postpone the trip until I was feeling up to it. My close friends and family were shocked when they heard what had happened. Most people didn't notice a thing. A few people said that they thought I looked tired. I felt terrible about breaking my foot on my wedding day. I thought that life was being so cruel to me. I struggled and suffered so much and couldn't believe that this happened to me on what was supposed to be the happiest day of my life. My childhood thoughts of life warning me that I dare not try to be normal and do normal things crept into my mind. How could I think that I deserve to rejoice and be celebrated by others? *You have SMA; you are not allowed to enjoy the normal things in life.* I found myself thinking of all the shit I had gone through. I endured a horrible marriage and spent ten years searching for my soulmate. That thief, SMA, was slowly stealing my strength, and once again, it tried to rob me of having a normal life. It tried to destroy one of the happiest days of my life. The message was loud and clear: "How dare you think that you can escape my wrath. How dare you think that you deserve to delight in the joys of life? I will never stop reminding you that you don't deserve to be happy." I was disappointed in God because I had asked him to help me get through the day without falling, and not only did I fall, but I broke my foot. I thought that He was abandoning me. I never asked for God's help again after that day. I decided that I should instead pray for strength. I prayed for the strength to get through life with SMA. I had to stay positive and think that it could have been worse. I could have broken my leg and not been able to walk at all. I could have been rushed to the emergency room and missed the entire reception. Although I was in pain the entire night, I got through it, and no one even knew. I felt like I was at war with an enemy residing inside of me. A battle between anger and gratefulness was fought in my mind. SMA was unyielding, but I was resilient, and I wasn't going to let it steal my happiness. I decided to see the incident as a victory.

    I remembered watching Kerri Strug win a gold medal at the 1996 Olympic Games in Atlanta. What made her win so amazing wasn't just her perfect score, but the fact that she did it with an injury. After tearing two tendons, she put the pain aside and performed an almost perfect landing off the vault. Not only did she win a gold medal, but the U.S. Olympic team won the gold as well. Afterward, she knelt in pain and was carried away. I still get teary-eyed when I watch that amazing moment in Olympic history. In this event in my life, I was a gold medalist.

We were finally able to go to Maui in mid-October. My foot was still a little sore and it swelled up on the plane. When we exited the plane, two Hawaiian women greeted us by placing leis around our necks. As soon as we left the airport, I felt like we were in paradise. There was calmness in the atmosphere. Everyone we encountered was pleasant. Time seemed to move slower. The rapid pace and urgency that I was accustomed to in New York were gone. As we drove from the airport to our hotel, I soaked in the warm sun and admired the views of the ocean on one side of the road and the mountains on the other. In the hotel lobby, a waterfall cascaded into a pool with live flamingos walking about. After we settled into our room, I quickly fell asleep, exhausted from the long trip.

The next morning, I realized that none of my shoes fit. Jorge found a pair of flip-flops with flowers on the straps for me in one of the hotel shops. I wasn't going to let a little swelling ruin my trip.

Lydia and her cousin were vacationing in Maui at the same time as us. On our first night, we all met up for dinner. Jorge and I enjoyed relaxing by the swimming pool while sipping on exotic drinks; we sunbathed on the hotel's private beach and went snorkeling. We went to a luau and marveled at the men dancing while spinning torches and the hula dancers. On our trip to Hana, we saw goats climbing the cliffs and stopped to take pictures of the many waterfalls cascading down the side of the mountain. We enjoyed the beauty of nature as we observed the scenery of exotic flowers and plants.

We took a helicopter ride over the island and saw waterfalls so magnificent they seemed to belong in a fairytale. The pilot informed us that the waterfalls from the movie *Jurassic Park* were filmed from our location.

During my days of hardship, when I was still in college, studying for exams and struggling to make ends meet, I had taken my boys to see the movie when they were only seven and eight years old. I remember being in awe when the camera panned out over the breathtaking waterfalls surrounded by foliage, thinking that it must be one of the most beautiful places on earth. I wondered if I would ever be fortunate enough to see a paradise like that one day. Peering through the helicopter window, I thought of how serendipitous it was to be flying over the same paradise seven years later. It was moments like these that SMA couldn't touch.

Chapter 10

Working

After the honeymoon, I returned to work. It was my fourth year of teaching, and my first year having an assistant to do the footwork of picking up the kids. It made it so much easier, but as SMA progressed, I had to get used to new levels of what was normal for me. I was at the district office for a speech meeting and twisted my ankle going down the stairs. It was a warning that I was getting weaker and should go down more slowly and with caution. Gone were the days of running or quickly descending. I found myself needing to hold on tight and go down one step at a time. At the same time, going up the stairs started to become even more difficult. There was an old freight elevator at the district office. Until then, I only used it to go up. It was on the other side of the building, which meant a lot of walking back and forth just to use it.

Although I tried avoiding stairs like the plague, I couldn't erase them from my life completely. When both elevators at my school were out of service or during a fire drill when they were turned off, I was forced to deal with an old, familiar hurdle. I found a new way of conquering the stairs. I held onto the left banister using both arms. If I extended my legs out behind me while leaning against the banister, I was able to get up one step at a time. I chose a back staircase with little traffic to perform my procedure to avoid anyone observing my struggle. If someone entered the staircase, I stopped and rested until they passed.

Eventually, I was allowed to go into the holding area (a room designated for students in wheelchairs or others with mobility issues) during fire drills. I became the designated teacher for the holding area on my floor. The rooms were designed to be fire-resistant and had windows that opened like doors, so in case of an actual fire, the firemen would climb up and help the children out. The other adults in the room were the paraprofessionals assigned to the children with disabilities. They often joked that they wouldn't mind being rescued by a fine-looking firefighter.

Life was busy as I worked full-time and ran a household while earning my master's degree. I drove into Manhattan to Hunter College on days I had classes. I had to adjust to my slowly weakening body and find new ways to deal with obstructions like curbs. I walked to the corners on the street where the ramps were. Sometimes using the ramp meant walking further from my car to get to it. Going up the ramps wasn't always easy either. I had to go slowly, especially if the incline was steep. If I was too tired to walk to the corner, I'd hold onto a car for balance when stepping off the curb. Although the special parking permit allowed me to park close to the building at work, I struggled more often to get from the car to the front door. Even with the permit, a delivery truck would sometimes be parked in "my" spot. I'd sit in the car, parked behind it, nervously waiting for the driver to finish delivering his goods to the bodega across the street, hoping it didn't take too long, causing me to be late.

I was overcome with anxiety on the days that we had meetings in other schools because there were unknown variables at different locations. The parking wasn't guaranteed, and even if the building was accessible, it often meant that I had to walk out of the way to find a ramp or an entrance that was accessible. The accessibility was designed more for someone using a wheelchair. It was more difficult for ambulatory disabled people. Once I had a meeting in Queens at a junior high school. When I arrived, I found a parking spot on the corner of the school. The entrance was in the middle of the block and there was a huge flight of stairs at the entrance. It was a cold, windy day and when I got out of my car, I knew I wouldn't be able to make it down the block and up the stairs. I looked around desperately and noticed a teacher standing outside directing students. I called out to him.

"Excuse me, excuse me. Hi, I'm here for a speech teacher's meeting. Is there a handicap-accessible entrance that I could use? I have a disability and it's very difficult for me to walk up steps."

"Yeah, there's one on the other side of the building. You would have to go down this avenue, it's around the corner."

"That sounds like a lot of walking, and if I drive over there, I might not get a parking spot." I answered. "Would you mind if I held on to your arm while I walk toward the main entrance and up the stairs?" I asked.

"No, I wouldn't mind." He answered.

When I got near the top of the stairs in front of the school, I saw one of my colleagues.

"There's one of my coworkers. I'll ask him to help me. Thank you so much. I don't want to take up any more of your time."

When I entered the building, there was another set of stairs in the vestibule.

Being off in the summers gave me the opportunity to make some extra money. I had worked in Staten Island at a school for children with severe disabilities the summer before. Many of the students were in wheelchairs, most were nonverbal, and some had multiple disabilities. I liked the staff and enjoyed working with a different population. I decided to apply for a position at that same school the following year. I was happy to see some of the teachers and therapists that I met the year before. Some worked there during the year, and others were from other schools, like me. I had met a speech therapist named Jennifer the previous year and was delighted to see her again. We shared a therapy room and materials. I told her that I had SMA and shared some of my story with her. I wanted her to understand if I had to walk slowly or if I couldn't help lift or carry things. One of my groups had two children in wheelchairs. I was pulling one child in his chair behind me while pushing the other in front of me to get them into the therapy room. It was kind of awkward, but the classroom was across from ours, so I didn't have to go far. One day during a fire drill, Jennifer saw me struggling to get both wheelchairs out of the building. She ran over to me and quickly took one of the wheelchairs from me and escorted the student outside. I never thought to tell anyone that it was too much for me physically and ask for someone else to take that group. I knew summer would go by quickly and I'd find a way to manage.

Parking was a challenge at this school, so when I couldn't find a spot close by, I'd park in an area in the back that had a "No Parking" sign. It was a designated area for the buses to drop off students. I parked right behind the sign, leaving the entire block behind me available for the buses.

One day on my way to my therapy room, I passed the security guard's desk.

"Hey, you can't park back there," she snapped.

"I can park there because I have a handicap parking permit that allows me to park legally in no parking zones. I parked close to the sign, leaving plenty of room behind me for the buses."

A couple of days later, I parked in the back again. I was in the cafeteria helping one of my students with feeding when I heard a voice yelling.

"Hey! You can't park back there. I already told you." I looked up and saw the short, stout security guard bounding over toward me.

"You better move your car, or it will be towed," she continued. The cafeteria became quiet, and everyone was looking at me. I opened my mouth, but before I could form any words, she screamed, "And I don't care if you are handicapped or not." She then stormed out of the cafeteria, leaving me speechless and embarrassed. The para that was assigned to my student looked at me sadly. "She can call the police, but I won't get a ticket, and I won't get towed because I'm parked there legally," I said in my defense.

I shared this experience with Jennifer and explained how the security guard was harassing me. She informed me that the guard also told her to tell me not to park there. Jennifer was concerned and suggested that we speak to the assistant principal. She accompanied me to the AP's office. He was a mild-mannered, petite man. I informed him that I had a disability and described the guidelines of my parking permit. I assured him that I was parking legally and was only parking there occasionally. I explained that I felt harassed by the guard and asked if he could talk to her. He listened and said he would see what he could do. We walked out of his office with the feeling that he was weak and wouldn't stand up to her. The security guard continued to make comments to other teachers about my parking. After a while, I decided to go up the chain of command and speak directly to the principal.

A couple of weeks prior, I was walking down the hallway and noticed the principal looking me up and down. She asked me if I was okay, I answered with, "Yes, this is the way I walk." When I walked into her office to make the complaint, I knew she remembered me. I began by telling her about my situation with the security guard. I also explained that I had complained to the assistant principal and that the harassment continued. I further went on to say that I was surprised to be treated this way, especially at a school that caters to students with multiple disabilities. She tried to make excuses for the woman, stating that she probably was unaware of my disability. I brought up how she herself stopped me and asked me if I was okay when she saw me walking down the hallway. She became combative and brought up that I answered with "That's the way I walk." I replied with, "Yes, it is the way I walk, and I don't explain my disability to anyone unless I feel it is necessary, and in the case of the security guard, I had disclosed that I had a disability." She answered with, "Well, you have a very slinky walk." Although I have been accused of walking sexy, in the case of the principal, she initially thought I was injured and now she's describing me as "walking slinky." It was obvious that she took offense to how I answered her that day in the hallway. She didn't seem to think that the guard's behavior was inappropriate. She offered no assurances that the harassment would stop or that she would speak to her. She went on to say, "Well, it won't happen next year because you probably won't be working here." This surprised me, because the supervisor of speech was the one who did the hiring of speech therapists. It was clear to me that she was threatening me with not allowing me to work there the following summer. I replied with, "How do you know?" She realized what she had said and tried to cover it up with, "Well, you never know what will happen." I left the principal's office feeling horrible. When Jennifer and I got back to our room, we were in disbelief. I began venting to Jennifer about the situation and when I looked over at her, I saw tears streaming down her cheeks. I was so moved by her emotional reaction. I knew what they were doing was awful, but I had kind of acquired a thick skin toward those types of people. Seeing her tears made me realize just how nasty they were, but it also showed me how kind and empathetic Jennifer was, and I knew there were more people like her in the world. The number of people who came to my aid when I fell, held a door open for me, offered to carry things for me, or did anything to accommodate me outweighed the mean and nasty ones. The next year, I decided not to apply for a summer position. I didn't need the money, and I wanted to enjoy my summer off, but I also didn't want to work in that school with those inconsiderate people.

In October 2006, Jorge and I bought a property where we would build our dream home in Pennsylvania. We planned to use it as a weekend, holiday, and summer home until we retired. As I sat there signing the never-ending paperwork, I couldn't help but remember the sad girl in the mirror, sitting on her bed holding her newborn in the midst of an eviction. She had come a long way in the last twenty years, and I was proud of her. With every accomplishment, I thought of her, and I healed her. Jorge and I had both lived in apartments our entire lives and we were thrilled to be acquiring the American dream together.

Christopher had joined the Marines three years prior and was stationed in San Diego at the time. Jorge, Andrew, and I moved in with Dad on Staten Island while the house was being built. The bedrooms were on the second floor of Dad's house. I knew it would be difficult, but I was up for the challenge and knew it would be temporary. I only had to go up once a day. On days that I felt extra weak, I waited for Jorge to get home to carry me up. It was a sacrifice I was willing to make to have a better situation in the future.

In June, I applied for a summer position to help with the extra expenses. It had been about six years since I had worked a summer job. I applied at the school I had worked previously, which would be very convenient now that I was living on Staten Island. I was happy to see that both the nasty security guard and principal had retired. The experience was pleasant without them. The teachers were so kind and understanding. They made sure that the kids on my caseload were near my therapy room. One of the teachers asked me if I'd like to work there all year. "We could make it very easy for you, if you transferred," she said. The speech supervisor asked me if I liked working at the school. I said that I did. I thought about transferring since the school was closer to where we were living, but I knew that I would miss my kids in Bushwick. It was a part of my life that I didn't want to change. I was blessed to be working with good supervisors and a caring staff. I knew my place was with them. I decided to continue driving forty-five minutes into Brooklyn rather than fifteen minutes away.

Waiting for the house to be built was an exciting time for us. We got to choose the style of house we wanted, as well as all the finishes. One of the main reasons I decided to have a house built was so that I could make it accessible for me. We had a ramp installed in the garage so I didn't have to climb any stairs to enter our home, and it would come in handy one day if I needed a wheelchair. I chose a model with the primary suite on the first floor so I wouldn't have to struggle up the stairs to reach my bedroom. There would be three additional bedrooms and a loft area on the second floor, which were for the kids. Chris was thinking of leaving the Marines when his time was up, so I wanted him to have a room to come home to. I also wanted a room for Andrew and one for Millie for when she visited.

In August 2007, the house was finished. It was such a great feeling to walk into a home of our own. With our jobs still in New York City and a ninety-minute commute, we decided to stay with Dad a couple of days a week to give us a break on the commute, but we spent every weekend in Pennsylvania. I had a total of eleven weeks off during the year, not to mention all the three-day weekends when holidays fell on Mondays. I had about ten more years left before I would retire, and having the house as a retreat was wonderful.

October 8, 2008, was a busy day like most days. It was a day of back-to-back therapy and a conference with a parent, social worker, and the psychologist. After the conference, I was on my way to the elevator when I stopped to say hello to a teacher. While engaged in conversation with her, I felt someone brush against my shoulder. I ignored it and kept talking, thinking that someone just got too close to me and would continue walking away, but it happened again. This time, the force against me was greater. I felt myself being forced toward my left, with my left leg sliding outward. I realized that I was going down but couldn't stop it. As I got closer to the floor I felt a pain in my knee. I remember yelling "My knee!" I was on the floor with my left leg bent outward, perpendicular to my body. Mark, one of the custodians, walked into the building at that very moment. He said, "I gotcha, Mama," as he rushed over to pick me up. I looked up to see who had done this to me and was shocked to see that it was a former employee named Steve. He had stopped by to visit and was trying to get my attention.

The first thing I said was, "Why did you push me?" He responded with, "I was trying to say hello." I know he didn't mean to hurt me, but whatever happened to tapping someone on the shoulder or calling their name? I could barely put pressure on my knee to walk. Luckily, the school nurse just happened to exit the main office moments after it happened. She and Steve helped me back to my room. I had to hold on to both of them to walk. The nurse stayed with me while Steve went to get ice. I tried to straighten up my desk, take attendance, and get ready to leave. After sitting with an ice pack for half an hour, I tried to get up but was unable to put any pressure on my knee. I looked at the nurse and said, "Why did he have to bump into me? I don't need this shit. I can't even walk." She just looked down, shaking her head. I wiped away the tears that ran down my cheeks and tried to compose myself. The assistant principal walked into my room and asked to look at my knee. She returned with an accident report and asked me to fill it out. The nurse wanted to call an ambulance, but I didn't want to go to the area hospital. I called Jorge and asked him to meet me at the hospital that I was familiar with. The nurse got a wheelchair and brought me to my car. She and Mark helped me get into the car, which was parked in front of the school. Since it was my left knee that was injured, I knew I would be able to drive myself to the hospital.

I parked near the emergency room entrance and called Jorge. He was just getting off the train and walking toward the hospital. When he arrived, I showed him how swollen my knee was and asked him to get a wheelchair from inside because I was unable to walk. He lifted me out of the car and into the wheelchair. An X-ray revealed a fractured tibia. My leg was placed in a knee immobilizer, and I was sent home on crutches and told to follow up with an orthopedic doctor.

After an MRI, I was informed that I had two additional hairline fractures, a torn meniscus, and a sprained ACL. I would need arthroscopic surgery to evaluate the damage and repair the meniscus. The surgery was done a week before Thanksgiving. Until then, I decided to stay at the house in Pennsylvania, where I would be more comfortable and stair-free.

I was in a lot of pain and unable to do things for myself. Jorge helped me into the shower. I was unable to step away from the water stream to lather up. I stood under the water and cried. I hated feeling helpless. I turned off the water, lathered up, then turned the water back on to rinse. I was unable to get off the toilet for the first week, but thankfully I was able to do it myself by the time he went back to work. Eventually, I was able to use the crutches to get into the shower. I left them in the corner so I could reach them when I was done. During the day, I could make tea and a sandwich. When I was done, I'd slide the cup and plate a few inches at a time across the counter until I eventually made my way across the kitchen to where the stools were. If SMA had taught me anything, it was to improvise and not to give up.

A couple of weeks after the surgery, I started physical therapy. My doctor suggested a physical therapist in Brooklyn. I drove into the city on Tuesdays and stayed at Dad's until Thursday for the sessions. Jorge carried me up and down from my room on the days of therapy. I stayed up in the room on Wednesdays, relying on Dad to bring me food until Jorge came home from work.

On the days that I traveled to New York, I'd get up at five o'clock in the morning to drive Jorge to the bus station, then go back home and sleep for a couple of hours before getting ready for my trip into Brooklyn. I used the crutches to get to the car, then placed them on the passenger side. It was very difficult to get into the car because I had to place all my weight on my injured leg to get my right leg into the car. With the car door against the wall of the garage, I was able to lean on it for support. Without the door against the wall, it would be too far for me to reach. Sometimes it took me a few tries to get into the car; the more times I had to try, the weaker and more fatigued my leg got. One time, my leg started trembling so badly that I felt like I was going to collapse. I knew that if I fell in the garage between the car and the wall, I'd never be able to get up. Not only was I terrified of falling and being stuck in the garage all day, but I was worried that I would reinjure my knee. The longer I stood there, the weaker I got. I had already placed the crutches on the passenger side and couldn't reach them for support. I was on the verge of my leg collapsing under me. I didn't know what to do. I began to cry and yelled out loud, "You can do this! You have to do it. You can't fall. You can't let yourself fall." I became desperate and my mind started to race. I looked down at the bottom of the door frame. It was close to knee height. I rested my right knee on it so I could take the weight off my left knee and give it a chance to rest. After resting, I tried again and was able to put pressure on the bad knee until I got my other leg into the car and was seated. Once I was seated, I was able to pull my left leg into the car. My heart was racing from the ordeal. I was exhausted and just sat for a few minutes before exiting the garage. I was now able to rest as I drove the ninety minutes into Brooklyn.

The therapy center had an underground garage, which was awesome because I wouldn't be able to walk from street parking to the building. On the way out, the parking attendant would bring my car around and help me in. The center was a couple of blocks from the Verrazzano Bridge, so I was about twenty minutes from Dad's house. I made the appointments late in the day so Jorge could meet me. If he had to work late, I'd wait for him at Dad's house.

When Thanksgiving arrived, I was determined to continue my tradition of cooking for my family. I was able to lean against the counter and prepare the food. Jorge helped by placing the ingredients in front of me. The kids helped with setting up and clearing the table, as well as cleaning up and putting the food away. I also hosted a dinner for the Christmas holiday. It couldn't have been done without the help of Jorge and the family, but I was proud that I didn't let the injury prevent me from enjoying the holidays as I usually did.

After being home for six months, I was eager to go back to work. I had been using a cane since the accident and thought that if I got back to work, I'd continue to heal and get back to where I was. My knee was still very swollen, so my doctor gave me a shot of cortisone. After the shot, I felt so much better and felt like I was ready to go back to work.

I returned to work at the end of March. With spring break coming up in a couple of weeks, I thought it would be a good time to get back to normal. I'd only have a couple of months until June, and then I could rest and continue to heal over the summer. The shot had worn off, but I was sure that by September, I'd be fully healed.

A year after the accident, I was still dependent on the cane and hadn't healed completely. I went back to the doctor and had another MRI. The results showed that the bones had healed but the meniscus hadn't. Another surgery wouldn't guarantee my knee being back to its normal state. I was faced with the reality that my present state would become my new normal. I also had to factor in the effects of SMA. I had to accept that I would never regain the strength that I lost. My knee was locking, stiff, and continued to have edema. Getting in and out of the car was getting harder and walking around the school was scary. Going up and down the stairs at Dad's house became even more challenging than before. I was unable to go down alone as I had before the injury. Jorge would go down backwards in front of me holding me by one arm while I held on to the banister with the other. Once we got down the stairs, there were four more steps in front of the house, and those last steps were sometimes the most difficult. I often looked at Jorge and said, "I don't know how long I can do this. I need to retire." I was very unstable and fearful of falling and reinjuring my left knee or injuring the right one. Jorge began driving me to work and helping me into the building every morning to ensure that I arrived safely. If I had things to carry, he'd escort me up to my room; if not, he'd leave me at the elevator. Once I was in the building safely, he'd take the train near my school into Manhattan. My assistant walked me to my car at the end of every day. When we had meetings on other sites, my kind colleagues were willing to help me. The colleague who helped me the most was Melissa. She met me in the lobby of the building that required a lot of walking and offered her arm for support. She walked me to my car when the meetings were over. She usually parked far away from the building to save money on parking. I insisted on driving her to her car as a small sign of gratitude. The last year and a half of working was only possible because of the kindness of others. As grateful as I was, I felt bad about needing help and losing my independence. Although they never made me feel like a burden, I felt like one.

Shortly after the accident, I was informed by my union that I could apply for a disability pension. Since the injury occurred on school premises, I'd be eligible for an accidental disability retirement or, as my lawyer called it, "the Holy Grail of retirements." If approved, I would bring home two-thirds of my yearly salary, tax-free. I decided to apply for retirement. I would have the paycheck, but I would lose the rewarding job that I loved so much. I would also lose that feeling of contributing to society and being the professional that I worked so hard to become. I feared that I would lose a part of my identity and a part of my worth. I would lose my friends and colleagues, and most of all, I would lose my beloved students—the students who brought me joy with their raw honesty, unconditional love, and eagerness to learn. I would miss touching lives, not only through their minds but also through their hearts. Teachers and therapists are more than educators; they are mothers, nurses, counselors, friends, and role models. I think the most rewarding aspect of teaching was making children feel good by helping them build their self-esteem. There is nothing greater than witnessing the spark in a child's eye when they accomplish a goal or seeing them look up to you and want to aspire to do well because of you. Although the prospects of retiring early would delight many people, realizing all that I would leave behind greatly saddened me. On the other hand, there was no way of knowing how long I'd be able to work with the injury and the progression of SMA. I felt that I had no choice but to stop working.

I applied for disability retirement in early December and kept it in the back of my mind. I loved reading to my students and savored every moment, sharing my favorite holiday and seasonal books with them. I helped them write about the stories and adored the drawings they produced. My bulletin board was adorned with their creative work. I tried to absorb each moment as I knew it might be fleeting.

I wanted to do something special with the prospect that it might be my last year. In the spring, I ordered live caterpillars so my students could watch as they metamorphosed from larvae to chrysalises and eventually into butterflies. It was something I had done a few years back and remembered how much the children enjoyed the experience. We read non-fiction and fiction books about butterflies. The children were so excited to come into my therapy room each week, anticipating each stage of metamorphosis. One group was present when one of the caterpillars hung upside down in the netted butterfly cage and shook until it was covered by its own skin, transforming into a pupa. Little by little, all the caterpillars were in the chrysalis stage. The children impatiently awaited the final stage of the butterflies' life cycles. One by one, each butterfly broke free from its cocoon. When one of the butterflies emerged, it looked like its wing was folded. I thought that it would open as its wings dried but the wing remained pleated.

The butterfly was never able to fly. It was able to walk and climb up the sides of the mesh cage. When it wanted to come down to feed on the orange slices that we placed in the bottom, it opened its good wing but fell clumsily against the wall and landed with a crash. Every day we witnessed the butterfly falling. It was heartbreaking to see the beautiful creature unable to fly. The children asked what was wrong with it. I explained that sometimes insects, animals, and people are born different. I talked about how some people are deaf and can't hear, others are blind and can't see, and some have trouble walking, like me. I shared that I couldn't run and had to walk slowly. When they asked why, I told them that if I tried to go too fast, I'd fall. For those who had difficulty with reading or speaking fluently, I said it was okay to have to read slowly or speak slowly, but I reminded them that they could run or do other things quickly. I explained to them that we all had different strengths and weaknesses. I said that the butterfly had to do things differently since it had a broken wing and couldn't fly.

Brandon, a student in one of my groups, had just started using a wheelchair that year. Brandon had Becker muscular dystrophy (BMD). He was in the fourth grade and had been my student since he was in kindergarten. When I explained that the butterfly had trouble flying the way some people have trouble walking, he smiled and said, "Like me, too! The butterfly is like me!"

After observing the butterflies for a couple of days, we had a freeing ceremony on the playground. It was a warm, sunny day in June. The children took turns reading lines of a poem that I wrote about butterflies before setting them free. When we first opened the netted cage, the butterflies didn't move. We patiently waited for them to fly free. Suddenly, a warm breeze encircled them, giving them a gentle push up and out of the cage. We watched as the butterflies soared high into the sky until they were higher than the school building and eventually out of sight. I listened to the children cheering and then looked into the butterfly cage at the broken-winged butterfly. I was saddened by the thought of how it was unable to fulfill its destiny of soaring to great heights and how it would never know what it's like to search for flowers and drink their sweet nectar. The children asked what would happen to the injured butterfly. I said that we would continue to take care of it until its life cycle was over. As we walked back into the building, I felt emotional as I thought of Brandon, the butterfly, and me.

I used to say, "Every day that I walk is a blessing, and every year that I work is a gift." I often wondered when my blessings would end. The game of "beat the clock" that I had felt ticking in my head most of my life had slowed down, as I had accomplished most of my goals before losing my ability to walk. I started to hear the old familiar ticking. It was a reminder that the threat of losing the ability to walk was approaching. Unlike Cinderella, who was warned that her carriage would turn into a pumpkin at the stroke of twelve, I had no idea when my luck would run out. I often worried that my fairy godmother would wave her magic wand and put me in a permanent seated position. I got the feeling that midnight was approaching for me and my dream of a productive life would soon end.

In June, my assistant helped me pack up my room for the end of the year. The walls and bulletin boards must be bare, and the bookcases barren in case rooms are painted or used for summer school programs. Things of importance are put into boxes, labeled, and locked away in closets or taken home. I was standing near the closet, giving her directions as to what went where, and took a step back. My leg bumped into the file cabinet, and I fell, banging my head against it on my way down. She looked at me, frightened. I assured her that I wasn't hurt and asked her to get the male para, Roberto, from next door. He walked in with a concerned look on his face. I smiled and said that I was fine and just needed help getting up. He smiled and picked me up as he had done a few times before. After he left, I looked at my assistant and said, "My ass needs to retire." She looked at me sadly. I hadn't shared my plans for retirement with her, but it was a way of giving her a hint, so she wouldn't be surprised if I didn't return in September. On the last day, I said my goodbyes and wished my colleagues a happy summer, knowing that it might be the last time I'd see most of them.

On a hot, sunny day in July, I had my retirement hearing. As I entered the conference room, the members of the panel watched me walk until I was seated. After I sat, I wondered if I'd be able to get up out of the seat when the interview was over. The chair wasn't too low, but I wasn't sure. I figured that I could always ask the lawyer to come in and help me. The three members of the panel questioned me about SMA and seemed more interested in it than in the injury that I had sustained at work. One of them was a neurologist and seemed to have some knowledge of SMA. They asked if I had children, and I disclosed that I had two sons and raised them alone for their first ten years. They seemed impressed with me when I explained how I went back to school to have a career to give them a better life and had worked for fourteen years in my current position. They asked how my injury has affected me. I described how difficult it was to get in and out of the car, how unstable I was on my feet, and that the injury had caused additional weakness to my preexisting level of atrophy, leaving me unable to walk without a cane. When the interview was over, I was able to get up out of the chair by holding onto the table. They observed me doing so and watched me as I walked to the door. I wondered what they were thinking. Did they think I was disabled enough to deserve the retirement? Would they blame the fall on SMA?

Before the hearing, I had expressed concerns that my injury would be blamed on SMA, therefore rendering it the cause of the fall and thus disqualifying me from the accidental disability retirement. My lawyer rebutted with, "But you worked for fourteen years with the condition. Had it not been for the person coming into physical contact with you, you wouldn't have sustained those injuries. You are a hero. It took a lot of strength to work with your condition." I always thought of a hero as someone who saves children from a burning building or takes a bullet for someone, and I knew that I was no hero by those standards. I believed he was being overly generous with the word. Looking back, I do think I was kind of brave to work while knowing that falling was inevitable. I was willing to work despite the knowledge that it would be difficult, because I felt that the good outweighed the bad. For all the days of struggle, for all the times that I fell, there were more days that I didn't fall. For every day full of fear and struggle, it was also a day of triumph. Even on my worst days, I was compensated with smiles and compliments from my students and coworkers. The rewards outweighed the struggles. When my students succeeded, I succeeded. It was worth every fall, every struggle, and every tear.

After the hearing, my lawyer asked us to wait outside. Jorge and I anxiously waited on benches in the courtyard of the building. When the lawyer joined us, he revealed that I was approved. He warned me not to tell anyone that I worked with until I got the official letter in the mail. My first reaction was elation. Jorge and I hugged, then I thanked the lawyer for his service. I stopped at Dad's house to tell him about the news on my way back to Pennsylvania. As I told him the results, my voice cracked, and my eyes got watery. It was a bittersweet moment. I got the Holy Grail of retirement, but I lost a part of myself. At forty-seven years old, I was officially retired. I was no longer a speech therapist. I was no longer a working professional, and I was no longer a contributing member of society.

Although it wasn't what I would have chosen, I had to see it as a blessing. I tried to think about it as one chapter in my life ending and another one beginning. I wouldn't have to climb the stairs at Dad's house during the commuting months, and we could live in our home full time. Jorge could commute via bus to New York, and there would be no more commuting and no more struggling for me. There would be no clock to set and no schedule to keep, only rest and relaxation. I was still able to walk, and I was grateful for that, but my level of independence was diminished.

Chapter 11

To do is to be—Socrates
To be is to do—Plato

Although my new situation was for the best, my identity had changed a bit. With my professional life in the rearview mirror, I wondered, *what will I do, and who will I be?* I needed to feel productive. I wasn't used to having so much time on my hands.

A month after retiring, Millie came to live with us during her last year of high school. I was happy to be available to her for guidance. A few months later, Andrew got married. His wife, Alisha and her five-year-old daughter moved in (making me a grandmother—a role I very much enjoy) while they finished earning their degrees. Chris left the Marines and came home to pursue college. My empty nest was full again. I enjoyed being in our new home full time. I enjoyed cooking dinners and decorating the house. I was happy to be home at a time when they all needed me. I babysat my granddaughter, Kharma while Andrew and Alisha were in school. I enjoyed helping her with her homework and playing games with her. I was keeping busy and feeling needed.

I tried to embrace my situation and focus on the good in it. I had a beautiful family and home. I found joy in simple things. In the spring,

I sat in my gazebo and listened to the sounds of nature from the woods surrounding me. I closed my eyes and meditated while birds sang, and squirrels frolicked through the leaves on the forest floor. I quietly watched the deer grazing on my lawn and the rabbits hopping along the line of evergreens at the end of my property. During the summer months, I enjoyed taking in the sun's rays, entertaining family with barbeques and water games. In the fall, I listened to the acorns dropping, soaked in the vibrant colors of the foliage, and sat by the firepit on not-so-chilly days. In the winter, I watched the snow turn skeletal trees into beautiful white monuments from my window. I began to feel as if I was part of nature and no longer missed my former landscape of concrete and buildings. I learned to appreciate the calm and the quiet atmosphere, and I no longer longed for the hustle and bustle that had once filled me with the feeling of accomplishment. I realized that I was where I belonged in life. I had already proven that I could do it all, and now I didn't have to prove anything to myself. Jorge and I were proud of the adults our children were becoming. As they left the nest for the final time to pursue their own lives, I had to teach myself that it was okay to do less and to rest.

During my career, I had episodes of what I thought of as nightmares because they only happened while I was sleeping. They started when I was a teenager and continued into my adult years. My heart would start pounding and I'd feel like I couldn't breathe. I'd try to wake up, but it was difficult to open my eyes. As my heart raced faster and faster and my breathing shortened, I thought I was going to die. I knew that waking up would be the only thing to stop the episode. Right before I felt as if I was going to pass out, I'd finally open my eyes. I awoke with a feeling of dread.

After I retired, the episodes stopped. It took me years to realize that the nightmares were nocturnal panic attacks. The stress and anxiety that I was feeling (worrying about being fatigued while walking, climbing stairs, and avoiding falling) as I navigated through my days accumulated and were released as panic attacks during the night as I slept.

I loved using literature to help my students improve their language skills and had always dreamed of writing a children's book. I finally achieved that goal and published a collection of books about the four seasons. I also began writing articles for SMA online organizations. I found a way to stay productive without the anxiety of commuting.

Chapter 12

 ## Hope

Through one of the SMA groups, I learned about a study that was recruiting adults with SMA. I thought it would be a good way to help the cause, so in August 2011, I joined an exercise study at Columbia University. As the doctor examined me, he said that a treatment and maybe even a cure was going to be available in the next three to five years. When he first said it, I was skeptical, thinking that he was being too optimistic or maybe he was gullible. I brushed off his statements and ignored the glimmer in his eyes. I had been reading for years that SMA was a curable disease and didn't want to get my hopes up. As time went on, I learned about a treatment being worked on. I listened as they excitedly spoke of the progress a new drug was having on fruit flies that were engineered to have SMA. After they were treated, the disease was reversed, and the flies were able to take flight. As the months went on, I heard that they were performing trials on mice, and like the flies, they were able to overcome the effects of SMA. A neurologist eagerly shared how piglets born with SMA that once dragged themselves around by their front legs were now running. Eventually, they enthusiastically disclosed that they were starting trials on human babies. I listened with hope and excitement but thought it would probably be years before the trials were over. It was difficult to keep my guard up. The hope started creeping back in. The possibility of stopping the progression of SMA and regaining some strength would be amazing. It felt good to have hope, but it was also scary. I remember watching actor Christopher Reeve on television after the 1995 equestrian accident that left him paralyzed. He was so full of hope. He hoped that he would live to see a cure for his paralysis. It is sad not to have hope. I didn't want to be hopeless. I also didn't want to be waiting for something that may never occur. I had to live between the reality of the disease and its progression with a glimmer of hope that I may one day be lucky enough to have some relief. I didn't expect to ever have a full recovery, but I would have been grateful with whatever help I got.

After the exercise study, I joined another study at Columbia. This one was for an experimental drug that was supposed to help with fatigue and balance. It was during this time that I met a woman named Terri. She was the first adult with SMA I had ever met in person. We were both ambulatory with SMA 3 and were both retired educators. She was fifteen years younger than me and used a scooter. She explained how much easier it was getting around without the fear of falling. She further explained that she was able to do more and that it had greatly improved the quality of her life. I knew it would do the same for me, but I wasn't sure if I was ready. I was afraid it might lead to more muscle loss. I discussed my concerns with Jacquline Montes, the team's physical therapist. She informed me that if I only used it for things that I usually don't do, it wouldn't cause more loss. She also said that if I continue to walk at home and only use the scooter for long-distance trips (that I was now avoiding), it wouldn't speed up progression but might increase my activity outside the home.

Walking through the mall was extremely arduous. The movie theater in our area is in the mall. I began to dread going to the movies (which is something that Jorge and I really enjoy). When I did go, I had to stop frequently to rest, and as my luck would have it, every movie we chose was in the last theater, making the trip even longer. My legs would burn from the walk, and it put me in a bad mood, thus ruining the experience. Once in the mall, I could only go to one store because I didn't have the energy to walk around. I thought about Terri and how she was going out and living her best life, and how I was avoiding doing things, so I didn't have to struggle. After a couple of months of pondering, I decided to get a scooter. I was fifty-one years old and thought that I had fought long enough. I was ready to struggle less and do more.

At first, I was self-conscious using the scooter, but then I noticed that people didn't even react to me differently. If they did, it was to hold the door open or apologize for being in my way if they obstructed my path. I loved being able to zip in and out of as many stores as I wanted. In the beginning, I'd go so fast that Jorge had to jog to keep up with me. It was great using the scooter for sightseeing. I could focus on the experience without being cranky from fatigue or anxious about falling and getting hurt. I felt a sense of freedom.

In the past, I thought that not being able to walk would be the end—the end of independence, the end of normality, the end of freedom, and the end of me the person that I see myself as and that others see me as. I fought so hard to keep walking. I wondered, *If I am unable to walk, am I defeated?* When I see others using wheelchairs and scooters, I do not see weakness or failure. I see strength and victory. I needed to see myself this way also. It is acceptance rather than defeat. I realized that life can still be good even from a seated position.

Getting dressed became harder. On some days, my arms crashed down as I tried to lift them up to pull my shirt over my head. When I felt extra weak, I rested my arms on the towel bar while lifting my shirt over my head. Getting off the toilet started to become difficult. I sometimes had to try a few times to get up. I realized this was a sign that soon I wouldn't be able to do it. I decided to purchase a toilet seat riser to avoid being stranded on the toilet. It wouldn't help me outside of my home but at least I'd be independent most of the time.

I used to squat over low toilets, but my legs began to tremble, or I'd have trouble pulling my trunk up to a standing position. I try to avoid drinking before I go out and I don't stay out too long in fear that I will need to use the bathroom and won't be able to. Walking through the house was also becoming increasingly difficult. I found myself holding onto the furniture more as I passed. I used the cane when I was feeling extra weak, and I maneuvered through the kitchen by holding on to the counters. I became like a baby again, cruising around the house afraid to take steps without holding on. I started doing less and less housework and used Jorge as my sous chef to prepare meals. The walking back and forth to get ingredients and cookware is very tiring. Once everything is set in front of me, I'm still able to whip up a good meal of fresh sauce and meatballs, beef stew, or my signature baked ziti, just to name a few.

My grandson Kevin was born in January 2016. Jorge made it possible for me to babysit him. I was unable to carry him in my arms while walking. I couldn't lift him up and put him in the highchair or lift him out of it, but I was able to feed him. I couldn't chase him when he quickly crawled around the house, but I enjoyed watching him take off. I was able to change his diaper with Jorge doing the lifting. I clapped and cheered for him as he ran around the living room in his walker. I delighted him in a game of peekaboo and rocked him to sleep. He fell asleep in my arms and on my lap more times than I can count, and for that I am truly thankful. He didn't know how weak I was. When he climbed onto my lap in my lifting recliner and let me hold him, kiss his beautiful face, and touch his golden hair, he had no clue that I needed that chair to help me stand. For him, it was a comfortable place to take a nap. He didn't see my disability; he only saw me.

There was a time when my disease progression was so slow that I sometimes thought that I could somehow beat the prospects of not being ambulatory. Maybe it was hope or maybe it was denial. As I began to feel the full wrath of SMA closing in on me, I could no longer deny it. My future was in the hands of brilliant strangers working long hours in laboratories. Their efforts will one day save the lives of thousands of babies and improve the lives of countless children and adults.

On September 26, 2016, the FDA received the application for approval of the first treatment for SMA, called SPINRAZA (nusinersen). We read that the decision would be made by spring 2017. Those of us with SMA Type 3 were worried that the treatment wouldn't be approved for Type 3 adults. We hoped to be included if the drug got approved. As I watched my grandson getting stronger and meeting milestones, I imagined myself meeting some of the same milestones again, with the help of a treatment. I laughed as I told Jorge that he may be clapping and celebrating while he watched me do things that I haven't done in years or maybe even things that I have never done before.

I felt like I was on a rollercoaster of excitement, thinking about the possibilities of treatment and fearing I might be excluded from it. Some days I read things that sounded promising, and other days I read about Type 3s being excluded because trials weren't done on adults. I felt hopeful and hopeless at the same time. As I struggled through my days, I told myself that relief was on the way; even if it wasn't approved for us all right away, it's coming. Even if I must wait for another year or two, it wouldn't be too bad. The knowledge that help was on the way made getting through the tough days easier. I told myself I should accept the way I am and be thankful for the strength I still have. I needed to focus on my family and all the gifts in my life. I try to think of something that I am thankful for every night before I fall asleep.

I feel guilty if I have not been productive. I need to do something every day, whether it's cooking a meal or folding laundry. Some days, I must force myself to sit down and rest all day. I try to read or do some writing on nonproductive days. I try not to feel guilty about not having energy. I'm trying to accept the way my body is now and not compare it to how it was. I'm starting to accept the fact that I may need to use my scooter or a wheelchair indoors one day. I'm so lucky to have such a good partner who is willing to do so much, but I wish I could do more.

On December 23, 2016, we celebrated Christmas early because it was the day that was most convenient for everyone. With Jorge's help, I made our traditional Christmas dinner of roasted pork with rice and beans. Everyone in the family looks forward to enjoying this meal. Our tree was dressed in clear lights and white and silver ornaments. Red and yellow flames danced in the fireplace, and merriment was made as Christmas music played in the background while we ate, drank, and talked.

Little Kevin clapped his hands, and we all rejoiced with him. After dinner, we gathered around the tree and began opening gifts. We were so thrilled to watch the baby open his presents on his first Christmas. We laughed as he played with the paper and empty boxes. Then we took turns opening our gifts and thanking each other. A Christmas movie played on the television. Although we weren't actively watching it, we'd catch ourselves saying our favorite lines and laughing at our favorite scenes. After dessert, everyone started saying their goodbyes.

Jorge was busy in the kitchen cleaning up and putting food away. I was so exhausted that I didn't have the energy to stand up and help him.

"Thanks for doing the cleanup. I'm sorry that I can't help. I must sit. I can't do any more."

"Don't worry about it. Go sit down and rest."

"What did I do to deserve you? I'm so lucky to have you," I said.

"No, I'm the lucky one." he answered.

"I'm not sure how long I will be able to host these holiday dinners," I said as I walked over to my recliner. It had taken me two days to recover from Thanksgiving Day.

I curled up with a blanket and became mesmerized by the flames flickering in the stone fireplace. When Jorge was done, he joined me in the living room. I smiled and said, "It was a success." He sat next to me and turned on the television. I picked up my phone to see which of the many pictures we had taken came out the best.

When I looked at my phone, I noticed that there was a message from my friend Patrice. We met in an online group for women with

SMA. She has SMA 3 and is a retired school-based psychologist. We connected right away and became close. It's vital to be able to connect with others who are going through the same struggles. I call her my SMA sister. We met in person that past summer while she was in New York on vacation. Anyway, I saw that she'd left me a message and that there was a missed call from her. When I read the message, it said, "SPINRAZA has been approved by the FDA for all . . . Merry Christmas."

I immediately texted her back. We were thrilled! I checked social media and saw all the exclamations from parents of children affected with SMA. They posted about their gratitude and hope that this drug would save the lives of their children. Mothers described their elation through tears of joy. The adults with SMA were just as happy, because we didn't expect to get approval and were thrilled at the prospect of getting relief. I texted everyone in my family about the great news. It was the best Christmas gift I had ever gotten . . . hope.

I had been fighting in a war like a soldier without a weapon or shield, repeatedly falling on the battlefield wounded and helpless. On October 19, 2017, I received my first treatment of SPINRAZA. I finally had aid in battling against SMA.

Today, there are three approved treatments for SMA, with many more coming down the pipeline. By January 2024, every state in the United States had adopted SMA as part of newborn screening. I'm elated to know that no child born with SMA in the US will go undiagnosed. Children will be able to receive early intervention, meaning fewer deaths and less suffering for babies born with more severe types. I hope that one day every country will adopt SMA into their newborn screening.

As the knowledge of SMA broadened, more information became available about the different types of SMA:

SMA Type 0, the most severe form of SMA, affects a baby in the womb. It can be fatal before birth and is almost always fatal within the first year of life.

SMA Type 1, the most common form, is life-threatening and can quickly lead to the need for breathing and eating support. Type 1 affects up to 60 percent of children with SMA and is likely to be fatal within the first two years.

SMA Type 2 typically impacts children before walking. They may be able to sit with support, but they are unlikely to be able to walk or stand without support, and they have a shortened life span.

SMA Type 3, or late-onset SMA, children may lose their ability to walk and other muscle functions, but some continue to walk well into adulthood. Individuals with SMA 3 usually have normal life spans.

SMA Type 4 is a rare form of SMA. Symptoms usually begin later, typically after age 30. People with SMA 4 usually only experience mild muscle weakness.

To learn more about spinal muscular atrophy, types of SMA, signs and symptoms, causes, and treatment, please visit the Muscular Dystrophy Association at mda.org/spinal-muscular-atrophy or Cure SMA at curesma.org. For those interested in the work of physiotherapists who are specialized in SMA, visit: stepinsma.org.

Chapter 13

Rising

As my activity level decreased, the falls became less frequent but more serious. My bones have weakened due to reduced weight-bearing activities. The day before my 56th birthday I fell and fractured my hip and patella. I had surgery on my hip the next morning. On what began as the worst birthday I ever had, Jorge managed to make me feel special by bringing flowers and cupcakes with lighted candles to my bedside. Jorge, my roommate and a nurse sang happy birthday bringing a bit of joy and normalcy to an otherwise bleak day.

After a week in the hospital and two weeks of rehab, I was ready to go home. I didn't want to spend the holidays away from my family, so I was elated when my doctor said that I was strong enough to leave and could continue physical therapy at home. I'd continue to need a walker and wheelchair for getting around as I healed. On Christmas Eve, I excitedly waited for my paperwork to be signed so I could be released. After Jorge and a nurse helped me into the car, I blew her a kiss. My eyes unexpectedly brimmed with tears as I became overrun with emotions. The care that I received from the nurses and therapists was truly humbling. I waved good-bye from the back where I sat with my leg wrapped in an immobilizing brace stretched across the seat. As Jorge drove away, my tears escaped running down my cheeks. When we arrived, the house was warm and inviting. I was surprised to see that the Christmas tree and mantle were decorated. I had told Jorge not to worry about decorating that year since I wasn't sure if I'd be home for the holidays. He confessed that he recruited our daughter-in-law, Alisha to do all the decorating while he was at work. I was filled with contentment as I snuggled with my cats in my recliner. On Christmas evening, my family came over with food and presents. That year my greatest gift was being home surrounded by family.

As I acclimated to life at home, I hoped to wean off the walker as I healed. Unfortunately, using a walker became my new normal. Although I lost the ability to walk unaided, I was thankful to still be somewhat ambulatory.

Nearly four years later, I fell and fractured my femur requiring a titanium rod to stabilize my leg. Once again, Jorge was there for me. He sat by my side every night after work, staying until visiting hours were over. Many nights I fell asleep while he visited because I was too medicated to keep my eyes open. When I returned home, it was still painful and difficult to walk and perform daily tasks, but I was happy to be home. Thankfully, Jorge was able to work from home to care for me until I was strong enough to do for myself.

Four months into my recovery, I fractured my tibia and fibula while at physical therapy. After being rushed to the emergency room for x-rays, we waited for the orthopedic doctor to assess the severity of my injury. I was hopeful. "Maybe they will put a cast on it, and I will be able to go home," I told Jorge. "It's probably not that bad," I added. When I was informed that I required surgery to stabilize my leg with another titanium rod, my heart sank. I didn't think I would to be able to handle going through another bout of surgery, hospitalization and rehab. I felt like I was in a living nightmare. My eyes filled with tears, and I looked at Jorge. "I can't do this again. I haven't even fully healed from the last one." I laid my head against his chest. "We can get through it again," he answered as he wrapped his arms around me.

I tried to think positive. "Maybe this time it might be easier. Maybe it will heal faster than the femur," I said. I hoped that I'd be able to go home in a week. Seven days after the surgery, I was still unable to walk. I was then transferred to a rehab facility. I was feeling miserable and helpless again, wondering if I'd ever walk again. Seeing Jorge was the highlight of my nights. On Valentines Day, he entered my room with roses, candy and dinner from a local restaurant. We closed the curtain around my bed, creating our own little oasis and watched a movie. No matter how grim things seemed, Jorge always found a way to make things better.

A week later, I took my first steps and knew that I was going to be able to walk again. Each step brought me closer to independence. After two weeks of intense physical and occupational therapy, I was strong enough to complete my healing at home.

After each injury, I fought away the dark thoughts that made me feel subordinate. I needed help with daily routines like brushing my teeth and washing my face because getting close to the sink wasn't possible while sitting in a wheelchair. Getting on and off the toilet, dressing, and getting in and out of the shower, as well as in and out of bed were also tasks that I needed help with. It took many weeks to *almost* get back to where I was. I lost a couple of abilities along the way. My new level of normal has changed once again. I still need help getting in and out of bed and in and out of the shower. I'm hopeful that on day I will regain those last two abilities. In the meantime, I revel in the knowledge that I conquered the pain and feelings of helplessness and hopelessness with my husband by my side, cheering me along. It wasn't easy. I cried, complained, and felt that I didn't deserve what was happening to me. I have mourned the loss of independence in some areas, but I'm thankful for the ones I still have. I'm most grateful to have such a patient and giving life partner.

Forty-two years after my diagnosis, I am still walking (with the aid of a walker). I believe the treatment is helping me fight. I'm hopeful for the other treatments that are coming soon. I am still rising above every moment of frustration, sadness, and anguish. I've learned to give myself grace. This is how I win the war against SMA. I rise by being grateful and choosing happiness.

When I was young, I viewed myself as weak because of the *falling*. I now view myself as strong because of the *rising*. I am no longer the autumn leaf. I am the tree whose fallen leaves are part of a passing season.

 # Acknowledgements

We get through difficult times and accomplish our goals not only because of our determination, but because of the people in our lives that give us help and encouragement along the way.

To my husband, Jorge Batista who supported me throughout this decades long journey of writing my story. Thanks for listening to it numerous times and reading the parts that were too difficult for me to read aloud.

To my sisters and close friends who patiently allowed me to vent about my hardships. You served as pseudo psychologists, allowing me to heal and make sense of the painful events in my life.

To Jenn T. Grace and the team at PYP for helping me get this book to the finish line, namely: Alexander Loutsenko, my project manager, for keeping me on schedule, and my editor Connie Mayse.

A special thanks to my niece, Ashley Hernandez: artwithlovebyash@gmail.com for doing such an amazing job creating the book cover art.

About the Author

Q.A.Batista was born and raised in Brooklyn, NY. She received her bachelor's degree in speech pathology from Brooklyn College and her master's degree in education of the deaf and hard of hearing from Hunter College. She worked as a school-based speech therapist servicing children with speech, language and hearing disorders.

She has published four children's books; Falling for Idioms, Cool Idioms, Spring into Idioms and Summertime Idioms. After she retired, she began writing about her experiences living with Spinal Muscular Atrophy. She is an ambassador for the mySMAteam.com health group where she offers support and advice to others in the SMA community.

The B Corp Movement
Dear reader,

Thank you for reading this book and joining the Publish Your Purpose community! You are joining a special group of people who aim to make the world a better place.

What's Publish Your Purpose About?
Our mission is to elevate the voices often excluded from traditional publishing. We intentionally seek out authors and storytellers with diverse backgrounds, life experiences, and unique perspectives to publish books that will make an impact in the world.

Beyond our books, we are focused on tangible, action-based change. As a woman- and LGBTQ+-owned company, we are committed to reducing inequality, lowering levels of poverty, creating a healthier environment, building stronger communities, and creating high-quality jobs with dignity and purpose.

As a Certified B Corporation, we use business as a force for good. We join a community of mission-driven companies building a more equitable, inclusive, and sustainable global economy. B Corporations must meet high standards of transparency, social and environmental performance, and accountability as determined by the nonprofit B Lab. The certification process is rigorous and ongoing (with a recertification requirement every three years).

How Do We Do This?
We intentionally partner with socially and economically disadvantaged businesses that meet our sustainability goals. We embrace and encourage our authors and employee's differences in race, age, color, disability, ethnicity, family or marital status, gender identity or expression, language, national origin, physical and mental ability, political affiliation, religion, sexual orientation, socio-economic status, veteran status, and other characteristics that make them unique.

Community is at the heart of everything we do—from our writing and publishing programs to contributing to social enterprise nonprofits like reSET (www.resetco.org) and our work in founding B Local Connecticut.

We are endlessly grateful to our authors, readers, and local community for being the driving force behind the equitable and sustainable world we are building together.

To connect with us online or publish with us, visit us at www.publishyourpurpose.com.

Elevating Your Voice,

Jenn T Grace

Jenn T. Grace
Founder, Publish Your Purpose

www.ingramcontent.com/pod-product-compliance
Lightning Source LLC
Chambersburg PA
CBHW032041150426
43194CB00006B/371